AF664425

Principle Jewels of Life to Enlightenment

Fragrance of the Unknown

Dr. Har Prashad

Principle Jewels of Life to Enlightenment

Fragrance of the Unknown

Dr. Har Prashad

BOOKS FOR ALL

Delhi

© Har Prashad

First Published 2015

ISBN 13: 978-81-7386-306-6
ISBN 10: 81-7386-306-7

Published By

BOOKS FOR ALL

(an imprint of Low Price Publications)
A-6, 2nd Floor, Nimri Commercial Centre,
Ashok Vihar Phase 4, Delhi 110052 (INDIA)
tel.: +91-11-2730 2453 fax.: +91-11-4706 1936
website: www.LPPindia.com
e-mail: info@LPPindia.com

No part of this book may be reproduced, stored in or introduced into a retrieval system, or transmitted in any form or by any means (electronic, mechanical, photocopying, recording or otherwise), without the prior written permission of both the copyright owner and the above mentioned publisher of this book. The views expressed here are those of the author and do not reflect the views of the Publisher.

Printed At
D K Fine Art Press P. Ltd.
Delhi-110052

PRINTED IN INDIA

DEDICATED TO

The Almighty, Cosmic Divine Power, Supernal, Silence and Formless Oneness; whose Blessings, Radiance, Continued Inspiration, Booming Energy and Silent Guidance that has graced me to follow the path of Peace and Enlightenment for realizing the Ultimate Truth and Self – Realization; and to be always being in Him and to be beyond Time & Space for ultimate mergence in the "Being", the Absolute.

November 2014 — Dr. Har Prashad

Preface

By the inspiration of Almighty and His divine grace, after life long spiritual engrossment the book on "The Principle Jewels of Life to Enlightenment— Fragrance of the Unknown" has been accomplished.

The book deals in depth understanding of multifold dimensions of human problems and their solutions through abstract dormant human sciences as conceived and perceived by the self analysis & experience as well from multifold valuable resources after deep study, which evolved my thinking and thus the principle jewels of life to enlightenment has been developed. This book is unique in many ways and directions since it contains the essence of various complex abstract subjects/sciences including: Things to Remember; Knowledge to be Absorbed; Self and Intrinsic Knowledge of Geeta; Virtuous Approach; Yoga; Health and Physiology; Beyond words; Deep Mystic Thoughts; Silence Mind; Small, Big and Great Mind; Avadoot Geeta; Crisis of Self; Sri Sutram and Sri Vidya; Approach to Deep Sadhana etc., which have deeply influenced me through out my life and finally the principle jewels of life to enlightenment and self realization has come to light.

From my early age, I was highly fascinated by the philosophical approach towards life, and with time I experienced the different creative approaches in problem solving through inner divine unison with self by various modes to follow the pathless path in life that has lead to precipitate and concise my thoughts in the form of this book, which I humbly consider the natural showers of His grace on the pattern of this present contemplation. The divine light channelized my thinking and inspired me to write the principle jewels of life to enlightenment—Fragrance of Unknown, which highlights the core essence of varied subjects of multifaceted dimensions for the overall self-development and dormant knowledge to tackle the various issues related to health, organization, self, social, and multifold problems of life by creative integral approach and self analysis leading towards the self-realization. Only the selected verses, expressions of evolved souls and perceived divine glimpses have been appropriately included in the various chapters of this book to make it self-explanatory. Almighty, the sacred force, alone is the force behind the expressions and expanse in all modes of His Own glory.

As I understand, no book covering many diversifying philosophical, dormant and abstract topics in this particular pattern; section wise; giving essence of many deeply concerned rare knowledge of human interest to enlightenment and self-evolution; and precise principle jewels of life to enlightenment and intrinsic values; has appeared so far. It is considered that this book will be vast treasure that will guide human being at the cross roads of life to choose an integral creative approach to pathless path for tackling various issues. Also, this will enlighten a seeker of truth to take up the vertical internal journey for mergence with the Absolute by overall self development and enlightenment.

In the light of the above, I would like to express that there is no end to conceive the depth of each word of the mysterious expressions and sayings, given in all 33 chapters of this book, which will certainly enrich the intrinsic values base knowledge of an individual to deal with the complex issues of human life besides implementing the principle jewels of life to self development, and finally for self- realization and enlightenment as the ultimate aim of life after enriching himself with divine qualities.

Finally, I would like to express my gratitude to the Cosmic Power, the Almighty, who has infused me to take up this divine accomplishment and boomed me with the source of untiring and inexhaustible energy by His Blessings, Radiance, Continued

Inspiration and Silence Guidance to nurture me all the time to follow and pursue the mysterious divine pathless path to be with the Self and Self-alone. Also, I acknowledge the silent participation of my wife, Darshan, son & daughter-in-law Poojan & Gauri, and daughter & son-in-law Shweta & Rajeev with little Kriya and loving Nimay to assist me to climb the ladder of divinity.

Har Prashad Ph.D.

Vancouver
June 2014

12533 South Surrey
28th Avenue
V4a 2n8
Canada

302 Cental View
Domal Guda
Hyderabad-500029
India

Mobile: 1-604-825-5139 (Canada)
Mobile: 91-9652013280 (India)
Email: har.prashad@gmail.com

About the Author

Dr. Har Prashad is presently consultant for Tribology and technical adviser to Rtec Instruments USA. He is retired Senior Deputy General Manager (Tribology) from the Bharat Heavy Electricals Limited, Corporate Research and Development Division, Hyderabad in 2004. He was consultant of Centre for Tribology Inc (CETR), USA till August 2011. He obtained an M.E. (Hons) degree in Mechanical Engineering in 1970, and subsequently, Ph.D. in Tribology. He worked with the Indian Institute of Petroleum, Dehra Dun, and with the Design Bureau at Bokaro Steel Ltd., Dahnbad, Bihar, before joining BHEL in 1974.

Dr. Prashad has published more than 125 papers in both national and international journals, reviewed more than 200 technical papers and many Ph.D. thesis. For many achievements, his name has been included in Marquis Who's Who in the world and International Directory of Distinguished Leadership published by American Biographical Institute. His bio-data is published in the directory of "Contemporary Who's who in 2004 & 2012". Also, "Scientific Award of Excellence 2011" has been awarded to him. Furthermore, for his distinguished achievements Tribology Society of India graced him with Life Time Achievement Award 2010 in the Seventh International Conference on Industrial Tribology-2010, held at Ranchi (Organized by Sail Authority of India under the Aegis of Tribology Society of India) on 4th December 2010. He is the Vice President of Tribology Society of India, and also Honorary President of Kriya Yoga Centre of Hyderabad.

He is the author of seven technical books and fifteen books on human sciences. The books are:

- "Tribology in Electrical Environments" published from United Kingdom by Elsevier Publishers in December 2005.
- "Solving Tribology Problems of Rotating Machines" published by Wood head Publishers, U.K, in February 2006.
- "Integral Approaches to Tribo-testing in Mechanical Engineering" published by CRC, USA in August 2009.
- "Behaviour of Rolling-element Bearings under Shaft Voltages" published by Lambert Academic Publishers, Germany in 2011.
- "Electrical Analogy of Different types of Journal & Thrust Bearings"
- "A System Approach to Mechanical Engineering Problems", 2011.

* "Anti-friction Bearings and Lubricants under Electrical Currents", 2012.
* "Solutions of Problems & Remedies of Human Life—A Path of Peace And Enlightenment" published in 2010 by DK's Books for All, India.
* "Japu Ji Sahib and Srimad Bhagavad-Gita – The Spark of Enlightenment", by DK's Books for All, India, 2011.
* "Spikes of Deep Silence by Silence and in Silence" published in 2012 by DK's Books for All, India.
* E-book on "Know Thyself - A Guide for Spiritual Aspirants" published By Yellow Bay of U.K. in 2011.

- "Dormant Human Science" published by Lap Lambert Academic Publishing, Germany in January 2012.
- "Mysterious Life Waves"
- "Unison at Core"
- "Retrieving the Immersed Subjective Science"
- "Multifaceted Approach of being Conscious and Creative—The Integral vision"

- "Life is Continuum with Discontinuities—Glimpses of Self in Self", 2012
- "Scientific Integration of Queries on Inner Human Life", in 2013 by DK's Books for All, India.
- "Life Extension through Manifestation of Consciousness—Transcendence of time & space with discontinuities", 2013.
- "Discontinuities in Continuities in Realm of Life and Evolution—Source of Subtle Wisdom", 2013.
- "Breath is Master—Health, Happiness and Transcendence through Breathing", 2014.
- "Improved Longevity of Life by Evolution in Consciousness", 2014.

Contents

1

Things to Remember

If we merely live on the surface of things; if in dealing with machines we make our selves into machines; we are surely heading for self-destruction.

******

Basic Capacity of human mentality is:

Ability to concentrate;

Accuracy of observation;

Retentiveness of memory;

Logical reasoning;

Judgment;

Sensitivity of association;

Creative imagination.

******

Evil is a self created shadow, that all your pains, sorrows, and misfortunes have come to you by a process of undeviating and absolutely perfect law; these have come to because you deserve and require them, and by first enduring, and then understanding them, you may be made stronger, wise and nobler.

******

To mentally deny evil in life is not sufficient, it must, by daily practices, be risen above and understood.

******

The foolish wish and grumble in life, but the wise work and wait patiently with selfless motive unattached.

******

It has been established that:

Self-purification gives health; Self-protection gives success; and Self-governing gives power.

******

Happiness, spirituality and harmony are synonymous.

******

The man of truth takes sword against himself only and not against others.

******

To be in the world and yet not of the world is the highest perfection.

******

The unchaste thought, impure desire, self-inclination and indulgence bring darkness and failure in life. However, more the man becomes chaste; the more welfare shall be added to him.

******

Virtue is seed, knowledge is plant and love is flower in a span of life.

******

Whenever the choice lies between one's profit and one's relations with others, one must prefer the later with discrimination.

******

Religion opens our mind to self-deception and it shall never be confused with perversion.

******

Man thrusts for knowledge but cares very little for truth.

******

Jainism was 500 years before Buddha and Buddha 550 years before Christ.

******

The simplest understanding of Moksha is the complete disappearance of ignorance when soul finds himself with Brahman (Almighty). Moksha means nothing but the destruction of the impurities of minds i.e. lust, anger, greed, delusion, pride and egoism. The mind becomes pure when all desires and fears are annihilated

******

Almost all the great artists, social reformers, poets, writers have drawn strength and inspiration by considering themselves as the instruments in the hands of inner spirit.

******

The man, who is not mentally unhappy whether the work is successful or not but performs action, nevertheless, still full of enthusiasm and perseverance, is a man of Satvika class.

******

A certain amount of tension and frustration actually increases a man's creativity.

******

Only after self-purification, the man becomes divine and his social status shall be measured by actual spiritual progress. He must be accomplished by divine faculties and not by stuffing the brain by merely information and data.

******

The maximum of liberty and minimum of restraint from outside should be the working formula for insuring the growth of real manhood.

******

Ours is basically a hierarchical, militaristic society, in which people are objectively obedient to their superiors, and inhuman to their inferiors.

******

Every thing takes longer than you think it will.

******

The moment you follow some one you cease to follow the truth.

******

Control of desires can control thoughts and actions as well as ignorance and error in us. Only desire less mind can concentrate on self.

******

Unction is a path of renunciation and knowledge.

******

As per Jain Philosophy that the plans ideas, intentions and schemes of a person, who is full of excessive passion, do not bear fruits or, if they do that, it is owing to the working of a "Karma" or foreign energy.

******

The success of the control of nature's finer forces that are not generally known depends upon chastity.

******

The success of Mantras depends upon chastity of mind. The mental state is more important than the vibration of sound.

******

Problems are always for overcoming and reconciling.

******

Things are being done because man as producer cannot afford "the luxury of not acting economically" and therefore can not produce the very necessary "luxuries" like health, beauty and permanence, which man of consumer desire more than any thing else. It would cost too much richer we become, the less we can afford.

******

A worker utilizes only 3.5% time in real production of the total available time in his life.

******

Gandhi Ji told that the poor of the world couldn't be helped by mass production. They can be helped only by production by masses.

******

Most essential for success are: Motivation, Knowledge, Capital, and Market.

******

Business is the institutionalization of individualization and non-responsibility.

******

Difference of opinion is the cause of unhappiness.

******

You do not love a man for his own sake; you love your own self in him and nothing else.

******

Matter is a manifestation of energy and energy is a potential mass. For a man his world of matter and his world of consciousness are practically inseparable and indivisible.

******

There exists antimatter in the depth of cosmos and collision of matter and antimatter results in their mutual dissolution and possibility of a piece of antimatter reaching the earth without a collision with matter on its journey, which is quite remote.

******

In Mohammedanism iconography and music seem to have no place. In Christianity dancing has not grown as an expression of religious sentiments

******

Gandhism is basically communism minus violence.

******

Three things that shape the world are: science, spiritual knowledge and literature.

******

Acharya is a violence prevention department where as Government police are the violence suppression department.

******

More brain and less heart start the violence.

******

If education is not expanded, people will remain ignorant; if it is expanded they will be unemployed. The choice is between ignorant and uselessness.

******

A slave has no obligation to defend his slavery. His only obligation is to destroy his bondage.

******

Communism was founded because it had ceased to believe that any ethical judgment would be regarded as obsolete.

******

For communists there were ends to judge. To Gandhi ji there were only means and each mean became the end.

******

2

Knowledge to be Absorbed

Universe is self-creating; self-dissolving; self manifesting; it is of infinite existence.

******

It is the weakness that is the motive powers in all evils; it is the source of all evils; it is the source of all selfishness; it is the weakness that makes the man injures others.

******

Jnana Kanda of the Vedas comprises of Upanishads and it is known by the name of Vedanta.

******

Prana and mind are complimentary of food. Mind springs out from prana.

******

One gets self-integrated personality through selfless service, japa, puja, Sandhya, meditation etc.

******

Knowingly ignoring the things is one of the attitudes of the spiritually advanced yogis.

******

Pure awareness or consciousness is a circle whose centre is everywhere.

******

The more we renounce and get over the negativities in us, the more purified we become in our minds.

******

Learning without thinking is a labor lost and thinking without learning is perilous.

******

If at all any one of us is meeting with obstacles either from outside or from within, they are all because we are not established in the truth.

******

Petty life of hurry, worry, excitement and competition will seem to you as nothing when compared to the everlasting life of eternal sunshine and bliss in the Ataman within.

******

Hirayangarbha was the only original teacher of yoga. Patanjali is only a compiler.

******

Thought is a dynamic force. It has weight, color, shape, size and form. It is caused by vibration of psychic prana or sukshma prana on the mental substance/body. It is very fine force. It is supplied to us by intake/food through senses besides inbuilt tendencies. Thinking is of four kinds:

1. Symbolic thinking,
2. Instinctive thinking,
3. Impulsive thinking,
4. Habitual thinking.

******

Concentration without purity of mind is not much of use. However, cultivation of purity of mind by self-efforts and concentration must go simultaneously.

******

Samadhi is of two kinds i.e. Savikalpa and Nirvikalpa. Savikalpa Samadhi where samaskaras are still there and not burnt, where as in Nirvikalpa Samadhi, samaskaras are fully burnt/fried.

******

Six basic virtues of human life are:

1. Soma — tranquility of mind;
2. Dama — self restraint;
3. Uparathi — renunciation;
4. Titiksha — endurance, tolerance;
5. Sraddha — faith; and
6. Samadhana — one pointed mind.

******

Shiva is awareness and Shakti is the creator. Shivlinga is the symbol of the astral body.

******

Snake stands for eternity or the concept of time. Kundalini power is beyond time. When manifested, it is subjected to time and space and it is like the act of awakening of the serpent. Kundalini rests in Muladhara. Goddess of Muladhara is Dakini or Savitri (red eyed and fearsome). Dev/God of Muladhara is lord Ganesh.

******

All past Karmas, human personality is symbolized in Swadhistanam Chakra. It is the stage of Hiran-garbha.

Brahma/Saraswati is the deity of Swadhistanam. One must be fully vegetarian for evolution of this Chakra.

******

Desire-lessens is a state of perfection and egolessness is the state of Godhood.

******

Energy is gained only by moral values and ethical values only.

******

Material life is nothing but an endless race to catch one's own shadow.

******

Religion without philosophy is a superstition.

******

Hanuman says — O Lord, at moments when I am steeped in my body consciousness, I am thy slave, when I identify myself with the mind and intellect i.e. as a jiva, I am a part of thee, and when I am in my swarupa, that is as the spirit, I am thyself.

******

OM is basically as AUM, where A stands for waking state, U as dream state, M as deep sleep state, and Turiya is a super conscious state.

******

Five basic constituents of our physical body have the capabilities as: Akasha.... Only sound; Air.... Touch and sound; Fire.... Sound, touch and form; Water... Sound, touch, form and taste; and Earth.... Sound, touch, form, taste and smell.

******

Enlightenment comes in flashes and if one is not sensitive and extraordinary alert, he may miss it.

******

The happiness is possible only in proportion to the amount of integration that the individual has gained within himself.

******

Social nature is good for doing Karma yoga. But it is extremely bad for practicing Dhyana Yoga. It makes the mind restless. Excessive work is hindrance in meditation. Work and meditation act as the acid and alkali on fire.

******

It must be clearly understood that there is no meditation in Samadhi. Vasana is a latent tendency and shorter the Mantra, the greater will be concentration.

******

Birth, death, hunger, thirst, exhilaration, depression are the six waves, which affect the Jiva.

******

A proper understanding of Almighty/Brahman is only possible when one lives in complete seclusion for a few years.

******

Spiritual man should not argue with others and not bother for name and fame. Also, company of worldly man is not healthy for a spiritual aspirant.

******

Do not be too much familiar with any one. Too much familiarity ends in rupture and enmity.

******

Pain/troubles/miseries open the inner eyes and inward journey is accelerated.

******

Philosophy takes its origin from pain; finds out the cause of pain and ignorance; and try to reduce it by the eradication of ignorance.

******

The man of discrimination remembers his sufferings. He suffers the most since he is neither Giyani nor worldly.

******

Even Brahma and Indira will be jealous of a contended man.

******

Hide yourself and do not show your skill and ability to others.

******

Don't expose the faults of others. Always bear insult and injury. This will develop your will force.

******

Fear of God is the beginning of wisdom.

******

Mind is the cause of bondage and liberation. Expansion of mind is Sankalpa. Sankalpa through its power of differentiation generates this universe. Sankalpa is only Samsara, its annihilation is Moksha. By abounding the pleasures of the world, you can lead towards Moksha. Time and space are just mental creation.

******

Realization is possible through intuition; intuition is feasible through meditation; through calmness; through desire-lessens; and finally through proper health and less eating; and one pointed mind; not mixing in gathering; being alone without in social circle and so on. There is no other way.

******

Peace, contentment, Sat-Sanga, deep contemplation and finally silence are the jewels of life achieved through meditation; these are to be guarded till the gates of Moksha.

******

If the lust for woman and wealth are vanished, all worldly bondage will come to an end; Atma-vichara/enquiry destroys the vasanas, thoughts along with worldly pains and miseries; and thus one will be free from birth and death.

******

A bath in Ganges, austerities and pilgrimage will only purify the heart but cannot help one to attain directly the immaculate Brahmin Seat.

******

The universe is nothing but expansion of thoughts. Thoughts of objects lead to bondage. Renunciation of thoughts leads to emancipation.

******

Religion has four parts namely: mythology; ritual; philosophy; and higher spiritual disciplines; of which meditation is the highest.

******

All laws being nothing more than the unity in diversity; harmony in heterogeneity; unison in diversity; all these are itself a phase of love.

******

Effect of concentration increases and is proportional to as the square of the number of like-minded people present.

******

The cycle goes on without a stop unless a man frees himself from it by putting an end to the cause of its beginning.

******

Ahimsa is a way of living where as Vedanta is a way of thinking.

******

Only self-knowledge, science and faith can lead us towards the universal peace, happiness, prosperity, and an end of suffering and hard ship.

******

When dead lock is reached in human affairs, someone has to make sacrifice if physical violence is unacceptable.

******

Buddhism and Jainism do not follow the rituals of Veda.

******

An ordinary mind is truthful when the words follow the facts. But the saint words are followed by facts. Such is the relation between saintliness and truthfulness.

******

The most ancient portion of Vedas is Samhitas, and the latest is Shasta's.

******

Educated Mohammedans are called Sufis.

******

Each work has to pass through three stages i.e. Ridicule, Opposition and Acceptance.

******

The Goddess herself lives in the houses of virtuous man as Lakshmi

******

Mother Kali is considered as the symbol of truth.

******

Every evolution is preceded by an involution.

******

A Sanayasin cannot belong to any religion; his is a life of independent thought; his is a life of realization; not merely of theory or believe; and much less of dogmas.

******

Rest and activity go together. Better you rest, nice you will work.

******

Fewer inhales and more exhale (1:2) is better for health.

******

Mind goes to the place of greater happiness depending on his direction and attitude (this may be healthy and right or unhealthy and wrong).

******

There are four types of men in the world: Rational; Emotional; Mystical; and Worker.

******

Each object in this universe is endowed with four characteristics: dharma means nature; karma as action; prema/love that binds to be together; because of this electrons are moving; atoms are combined making molecules and so on; and Guyana is to know; not through head but by all senses including consciousness that presents all over the body and beyond the body.

******

There is a degree of knowingness present in the entire creation. The degree varies like the level of love in the universe. By increasing the sense of knowingness reduces Karmas/action performed.

******

Mind selects the womb as per impressions. So last thought of the mind before death is more important.

******

In closely knitted family, children have same behavior as grand parents.

******

Jailor and prisoner are both in jail but jailer is like Jiwan Mukta i.e. liberated, who can come and go from jail but not the prisoner.

******

Truth is not linear. It is multidimensional. Every point is connected with every other point.

******

There are many types of Karmas including individual, family, social etc. One cannot pinpoint, which Karmas bring what effect at the deep level. It is almost impossible because it is so enormous.

******

3

Self Knowledge

The vibrations of vital breath excite desires and feelings in the heart. If it is suppressed, the mind rendered quite. But it cannot be suppressed permanently; it can only be controlled for a time being. However, frequency of vibrations of Prana by breath is generated by food, work, space, time, causation, samaskaras and other so many factors.

******

Energy lies in atoms not in molecules and still more precise in electrons. Similarly like electrons, if more refined is thought concentration, it will have higher value of energy.

******

After one overcomes impure awareness state of restful alertness, only then the great momentum is achieved.

******

Not the desires but the unfulfilment of desires gives the dissatisfaction.

******

Getting powers without purity of mind is a hindrance in success.

******

The self must be heard, then to be reasoned and finally it is to be meditated upon.

******

As we make our life more pure and noble, we enjoy more beauty and eternal joy.

******

Meditation suppresses/suspends breath and controls pranas. By turning the tip of the tongue inside, meditation becomes easy.

******

No object gives pleasure if one is contended.

******

If mind is fully under control and one pointed, it ceases to exist. Then only one enjoys infinite bliss. And if one is not agitated under tarrying circumstances, he is fit to enter the Moksha. Here thoughts and Maya/illusion end. In addition, when mind is absorbed in the self, it is death for mind and start of the source of self-realization.

******

Even great Devas are subject to the condition of their bodies. When the beginning-less emotions and desires are exhausted then only state of perfect peace comes.

******

Only after getting Samadhi, one can live without eating and sleeping.

******

If you do every act mindfully and consciously, that becomes Karma yoga. It is only Karma when it is done mechanically.

******

Always psychological satisfaction is richer than physical gratification.

******

Unless inward/self life is mastered, outer world does not give satisfaction.

******

Revolt is the very spirit of an evolutes, the majority are generally humble adopter to every situation.

******

If the words express something different from what mind declares, there will be a dangerous shattering in his inner personality. There should be healthy harmony between mental moves and vital expressions.

******

There are three groups of obstacles in the divine path. They are:

1. God sent…lightening, thunder etc.
2. Phenomenal…fire, flood etc.
3. Subjective… inertia, lack of faith, etc.

In most of the cases subjective hindrances is the major cause.

******

Changes take place only on the changeless ground. We define creation/changes in terms of time, which in its turn is a created/ changed factor.

******

The Vasanas or mental impressions in totality are the cause for creation of changes in the self-life and our outward world.

******

Ishwara/Almighty is compelled to create a world determined by the texture and quality of vasanas/mental impressions that are to see their fulfillment in the world to be created.

******

In conscious sleep, the gross and subtle world of the waking (consciousness) and dream (sub consciousness) merge into our selves. And while we are in a physical sleep there is, as it were, a pralaya (dissolution) of our world.

******

Loka does not mean the world but it is field of experience.

******

According to Shiva, the camp headquarters of the self in the waking state is in the right eye, in the dream state it is in the throat, and in the deep sleep state it is in the hear-space. At the throat a kind of over centralization of the dream ego exists, and it is pointed out that in the deep sleep state individualistic personality folds up its nervous impressions and comes to dwell in the heart space.

******

When emotion over power the thoughts during interaction, ideas get flared up in to language to its white heat of intensity, without grammar and any rules.

******

Man of self realization lives in his own infinite experience of bliss; absolute in himself; desiring nothing; wanting nothing; expecting nothing; beyond all finite imperfections and miseries.

******

Without purity of mind, even the study of Vedanta is like jumping high with small legs and breaking them.

******

It is very important to perceive that even if you imagine that nothing exists, there will be space and you have to transcend the space also for knowing the self.

******

The centre of moon in human body is Ajna Chakra and centre of Sun is at Manipura. Prana is connected with Sun, and mind is connected with moon. Manipura Chakra, when aroused emits Soma, which can be directed upwards up to Ajna Chakra i.e. Kautash Chaitanaya. Vipreetkari Mudra is basically to bring Sun upwards and Moon down wards.

******

Ram Mantra is for householders; Swadhyay is a continuous awareness; and Kundalini awakening is primarily for peace and knowledge; Followers of dharma in real sense are indifferent to praise and blame; and after self – realization, it becomes clear to the aspirant the location of five Pranas in the physical body i.e. Prana, Apana, Vyana, Samana, and Udana.

******

Yoga is the one comprehensive process by which a man ascends in the scale of life by performing acts, which are expressions of a dynamic personality based on the complete co-ordination of all his powers.

******

The greatness of a man is not in what he does but what he was and what he is now.

******

The mind becomes rebellion if more pressure of Will is put on the mind.

******

Sublimation requires the highest laborious affords into a higher unity.

******

It was in daily life that spirit is to be glimpsed. Life is not to be taken as struggle but as a fulfillment.

******

True service of a man is with emotion and spirituality.

******

Gayatri Mantra depicts that let us meditate on Ishwara and His glory, who has created this universe, who is fit to be worshipped and who is the remover of all his sins and ignorance. May He enlighten our Buddhi?

******

A whole man will be truly in touch with the centre. His touch will surely give the inner clarity.

******

Four aims of life are: Dharma; Artha; Kama (desires); and Moksha.

******

A spoken world is but a gross manifestation of subtle world, and subtle word is a manifestation of the causal word.

******

According to Vedanta philosophy, everything is matter, which is not pure consciousness or spirit.

******

The sheath of bliss is the same as the causal body in which he remains in deep dreamless sleeps.

******

Renunciation simply enhances your powers, takes away anxiety and fear, and makes you fearless and happy.

******

The mind should be subjected to the laws of statics and body subjected to the laws of dynamics. Body at work and self at rest.

******

Co-operation is nothing but manifestation of love.

******

Secret of success is: work; self sacrifice; self forgetfulness; universal love; cheerfulness; fearlessness; self reliance.

******

One must have the heart of Christ, brain of Shakespeare, and mind of Plato.

******

The more you succeed in taking off the Burden of thoughts from your shoulders, the stronger you will feel.

******

It is not your duty to worry or hurry about any business. Your only occupation or duty is to keep your self, self contained, self poised and self pleased.

******

For Nirvana:

1. Mind is to be free from passions and evil thoughts;
2. Sincerity and single point mind;
3. Equanimity and being mindful;
4. Beyond the duality of pleasure and pain.

******

By one's own efforts, by eternal vigilance and by following the laws of psychology that one can liberate himself.

******

MAYA means MA—- not and YA— that, i.e. not that.

******

Vedanta tells you that in your dreams, it is you yourself that appears as the object on one side and the subject on the other. So, you are the object and you are the subject.

******

If the Causal body were satisfied with the suggestion of Godhead, then the man is bound to be a prophet.

******

Pains and sufferings are blessings of this world. If there were no pains and sufferings, there would be no progress.

******

Your economic life, social life, your aesthetic life can be secured only when you turn to be a spiritual ideal.

******

Consciousness is Brahman/Almighty. It means that the individual consciousness; the centre of human personality; is not different from the supreme consciousness that manifests and sustains the universe.

******

To become a philosopher is to become transformed in life, renewed in mind and baptized in spirit.

******

When heart becomes purified by charity and sacrifices, there arises a hunger for knowledge of Almighty/Brahmin.

******

There are five debts, which shall be repaid:

1. To Gods .... By performing sacrifices;
2. To Sears......... By devotion;
3. To Pitras/departed souls... By praying for them;
4. To Man............. By love and sympathy;
5. To Lower Creation...By food and drink;

******

All existence is in the self and self is there in all existence.

******

Perfect observance of moral principles and perfect self-control are the only means by which the veil of ignorance can be removed.

******

Rare and blessed is the combination of these three i.e. human birth, desire for freedom and association with a holy man.

******

The yogic chakras in the body are categorized as:

Muladhara as Tamas;

Swadhisthanam, Manipura and Anahata as Rajas;

Vishudhi and Ajna as Satvik.

******

Basically Chakras are visualized, and are placed where nerves and muscles unite. Ajna Chakra is a place of command.

******

To control anger, one must meditate on Navel centre.

******

The braves are always having moral value. Cowards are those, who are weak, commit sin and speak lies.

******

The secret of life is not enjoyment but education through experience.

******

Satyam, Shivam, Sundram are energy, love and beauty.

******

Seek ye first the kingdom of God and His righteousness and all other things will be added to you.

******

He, who desires for a comfortable and nice life and at the same time, wants to realize the self is like a fool.

******

4

Deep Intrinsic Knowledge of Geeta

Man should be active, meditative, devotional and at the same time posses the knowledge of the self.

******

If among greatest activity, you find greatest peace, you are a yogi.

******

Thinking of objects; attachment to them; are built in qualities; formed in a human mind. From their attachment grows longing and from longing anger grows.

******

Insistence on the performance of Svadharma or one's own duty, in the spirit of yoga, is indeed often met with knowledge but this insistence looses much of its force with the growth of higher deep wisdom and knowledge.

******

Duty of one state of life, in one set of circumstances, will not and cannot be that of others.

******

Swadharma should be taken as per the state of growth.

******

Thoughts are also Karmas; so many karmas are not chaste.

******

Every Karma is the seed of other karmas hence karma is both caused and its affect.

******

Karmas are of three types:

1. Kriyamana.........Deeds of present life;

2. Samchita............Stored up Karmas;

3. Prarabdha.......... Stored up Karmas of past.

******

Karmas are attached to mind and not to real self, and knowledge of the self, burns the karmas of man. Work for the work sake purifies the self.

******

He, who, restraining the organs of action, sits with revolving in the mind thoughts regarding objects of senses, he is of deluded understanding, is called hypocrite. And roaming mind carries away one's own peace.

******

When man renounces all desires, satisfied in the self-alone by the self, then he is said to be of steady wisdom.

******

He who sees inaction in action and action in inaction, he is intelligent among men; he is yogi and doer of all actions.

******

Yogi must live in the world but world must not live in him.

******

Do every thing as worship to God.

******

Ignorance and delusion are characteristics of unregenerate mind.

******

Only when mind has become one pointed and concentrated upon God, he shall be filled with righteousness. And blessed are they, who bear hunger and thrust after righteousness they shall be certainly filled.

******

All the previous impressions must be dissolved for the mind to become pure.

******

Truth cannot be originated, it exists. You know the truth and you will be free.

******

Ethical life is the foundation of spirituality.

******

Does not compromise with ideals and principles but opinion shall be welcomed?

******

Truly spiritual man will never plan. He always says, "If the lord will..."

******

Never to offer violence under any circumstances, but it does not mean that one should not resist evil.

******

Your own nature will drive you to act.

******

Practice of forgiveness is the fundamental importance for spiritual aspirant. This will raise him above the ego, which obstructs the vision of God.

******

Spirituality and sadness does not move together.

******

The main purpose of life is to attain abiding bliss in the midst of fleeting pleasures of life.

******

Those who dwell on the faults of others, develop the same faults themselves in the subconscious mind.

******

To be found of learning is near to wisdom, to practice with vigor is near to benevolence (kindness) and to be conscious of shame is near to fortitude (endurance). He, who knows these three things know how to cultivate his own character; he knows how to govern other man; knowing how to govern other man; he knows how to govern the kingdom with its states and families; he is indeed virtuous.

******

To nourish the heart there is nothing better than to have a few desires.

******

Knowing one's own nature, one can learn/study heaven.

******

Spiritual and material in their origin are one and same. The sameness is a mystery; the mystery of mysteries.

******

Leave all things to take their natural course and do not interfere. Keep behind and you shall be kept up. Keep out and you shall be kept in.

******

Only from subjective knowledge, it is possible to proceed to objective knowledge. The subjective is consequence upon the objective.

******

Religion is rel (l) igio—religio means relationship, a kind of relation /communication between human and superhuman being as per Greek word that means scrupulous observation of omen and performance of rituals or realized inwardly.

******

Those who refuse to be diluted by their brighter hours will not suffer so greatly in their darker one.

******

The Vedanta tells that no person can harm us or wrong us unless there is some trouble within ourselves.

******

It is because of bad habits that self-control becomes difficult otherwise it is very simple thing.

******

Alteration of external life is virtually a change of internal consciousness.

******

He, whose, aim is the happiness of others; is virtuous; he, whose aim is God, is great.

******

The Wise man seeks death all his life and therefore does not fear death.

******

He, who renounces when he is not yet ripe for it, only creates new bonds for himself.

******

True renunciation is in the mind only and mental obstacles should be there where ever you are until the time is not reached.

******

The expression "It is breath taking really means it is thought taking" since the source of thought and breath is the same.

******

To crush all thoughts at their source is called Vairagaya (dispassion)

******

Contemplations are more effective than silent incantation and silent is more effective than uttered.

******

All sufferings of men are right as effects, their causes being the mistake of ignorance.

******

As per divine law, there is a survival of the Best. Survival of fittest revolves itself into moral principle. Fittest of survival is for selfish persons and not for the best. The best does survive and therefore pity, passion and love cannot be overthrown.

******

A physical pain is a protector of man's body, so mental pain is a protector of his mind and of his life.

******

Suffering of man indicates that divine law has been arrested. It is always the effect of wrong thoughts. The sole and supreme use of sufferings is to purify to burn out all that is useless and impure.

******

He, who studies how to become faultless; who strives to be pure hearted; who aims at the possession of a calm, wise and seeing mind; engaged in the most sublime task that men can undertake; and the results of which are perceptible in a well-ordered, blessed and beautiful life; is a divine man from the core of his heart.

******

Seed, tree, blossom and fruit are the four-fold order of the universe. Similarly thoughts blossom the deeds, deeds bear the fruits of character and destiny.

******

Life in totality starts from the mind.

******

The outer is molded and intensified by the inner and not vice versa.

******

Practice always precedes real knowledge.

******

Where there are wrong conditions of mind, there is a bondage and unrest, and where there are right conditions of mind there is freedom and peace.

******

Temptations are never overcome by unprepared fighting. Sin and temptation disappear when right understanding is developed.

******

Truth, patience can be increased by discipline only. And the courage of patience is greatest.

******

Once material consideration begins to dominate the mind, self-mastery is quickly lost; while one's grip on life visibly weakens.

******

A man is not rightly conditioned unless he is happy, healthy and prosperous being. And these are the results of harmonious adjustments of inner with the outer surroundings.

******

Conditions are for our progress only. However, we don't understand and realize them.

******

Yagna means an act directed to the welfare of others, done without desiring any return for it, whether of temporal or spiritual nature.

******

He, who bears enmity towards non; he who stands impartial and is free from attachments and serves me selflessly; he who dedicates to me all that he does; he who is filled with devotion to me; all enduring, free of passion and desires, full of love; such a devotee becomes an instrument in the hands of the Lord. This is the essence of the Geeta's teaching.

******

5

Virtuous Approach and Intrinsic Knowledge

Every time you feel annoyance and anger avoid interaction with others, especially with those depended on you.

******

There is no greatness than simplicity, goodness and truth.

******

Truth shall be in very breath of our life. Thought, word and deed shall be with true knowledge so as to be always in peace.

******

Brahmcharya is basically combination of Charya and Brahma i.e. conducts to follow the truth.

******

Possession without need is also a sought of stealing.

******

Civilization consists not in multiplication of wants but in deliberate and voluntary reduction of wants.

******

Outer circumstances shape itself according to inner core thinking.

******

Men do not attract that which they want, but that which they are.

******

As you alter your thoughts towards somebody, people will alter towards you. Whole world is connected with electromagnetic communication; we don't know it and don't feel it.

******

Selfish thoughts give and create distress circumstances where as unselfish thoughts give prosperity.

******

Man can only choose thoughts and not circumstances. Thought changes circumstances. Even thoughts depend on body conditions and finally it boils down to food habits besides in built tendencies.

******

Impure thoughts if physically indulged with, soon shatters the nervous system.

******

All that man achieves or fails to achieve is a direct result of his own thoughts. By refining the thoughts, only one can rise.

******

Self-control is strength, right thought is a mystery and calmness is a power.

******

If we treat others with kindness, forgiveness and gentle consideration, we can find that people in general are intrinsically good that they will heap kindness in reciprocation.

******

Perfection of conduct is the Christ preaching. There is no religion outside conduct.

******

Whilst a man cherishes lust, hatred, pride, vanity, self-indulgence, covetousness, he can do nothing significant.

******

Moment we get rid of attachment of the body, all fear will disappear.

******

If a man induces hunger by exercise, why should it not assume the form of productivity? This may boost the prosperity.

******

One should treat life properly as duty to live rather than as an indulgence in various undue activities.

******

Joy depends on our attitude of life.

******

Knowing is knowledge; seeing is religion; and becoming is spirituality.

******

What we need; our nation needs; or world needs; it is nothing else than the character.

******

A self- realized will always say that as for me, all I know is that I know nothing.

******

Hope is the greatest misery, despair is the greatest happiness.

******

The following is conceived with deep understanding:

In wealth there is a fear of poverty;

In knowledge there is a fear of ignorance;

In beauty there is a fear of ego;

In fame there is a fear of backbiters;

In success there is a fear of jealousy;

Even in the body there is fear of death.

******

He loses the goal, which chooses the pleasant. However, to be good is always good.

******

If there is God, you have Him being good. If there is no God, being good is good.

******

After any happiness, there comes misery.

******

One fails to attain realization if there be but a slight defect in the body.

******

Sattva binds through the search of happiness and knowledge; Rajas bind through desire; and Tamas bind through wrong perception and laziness.

******

6

Human Health and Physiology

Disgust, excitement, fear, anxiety, anger, fatigue, pain, injury will stop the movement of digestive track.

******

Fatigue dried up all the digestive secretions and so sometimes foul smell of undigested food appear in the stool.

******

If the food is not properly assimilated and natural function of body do not work properly, then that thing becomes the root of all evils.

******

Cause of disease is basically because of biologically wrong unnatural food and by each ounce of over nourishment only.

******

Man in perfect health should exhale fragrance.

******

When much waste is in circulation system, you will feel weak and experience bad dreams.

******

Knowledge leads to power and power leads to control and manipulation of forces of nature enabling man to condition his life and environment with deliberation.

******

Sucking digests milk. It is digested only in mouth and not by gulping.

******

7

Perfection of Yoga

No one can become a yogi unless he renounces the desire for sense gratification.

******

The spiritual platform is absolute. There is no question of becoming tired on the spiritual platform.

******

Krishna does not say that there is dreamless sleep, although one may not remember it. One, who dreams so much while sleeping, cannot properly execute yoga.

******

It is a duty of the yogi to always remain alone. It is not possible to concentrate on the super soul except in a secluded place.

******

As long as we have material body, sex desire will be there since we are born through sex and sex is there in each cell of ours.

******

If one wants to engage in yoga at home, then he has to make certain that his other engagements are moderate. He cannot spend long hours of the day working hard to simply earn a livelihood. One should work very moderately, eat very moderately, gratify senses very moderately, and keep his life as free from anxiety as possible. In this way practice of yoga may be successful.

******

Mind should be friendly in control but not suppressed. This is of success in yoga. Mind should not be agitated and it must be made friend.

******

It is not that the action is different, but there is transfer of consciousness from thinking of acting for senses to thinking of acting for Krishna.

******

The more we increase material enjoyment, the more we become entangled in the world, and the more difficult it becomes to get free from material entrapment.

******

We have to raise ourselves to the spiritual standard by ourselves and no body else can help except giving the verbal guidance.

******

One, who is absorbed, is free from all duality and false designations.

******

So for as one strives to get out of bodily conceptions, however not out of body but only out of bodily conceptions, he has to learn to tolerate duality of pleasure and pain, and so on.

******

Jnana means theoretical knowledge where as Vijnana means practical knowledge. A person can only be satisfied if there is Jnana and Vijnana side by side.

******

If one is self-controlled, he is not attracted by the material glitter and he sees everything including pebbles, stones or gold as the same. And a person is said to be still further advanced when he regards all the honest, well-wisher friends and enemies, the envious, the pious, the sinner and those who are indifferent and impartial with an equal mind.

******

The man, who is engaged in auspicious activities, does not meet with destruction either in this world or in the spiritual world. One, who does well, is never overcome by evil.

******

Even if one cultivates only little bit of real spiritual knowledge, he will never fall down into the material whirlpool.

******

To adopt real spiritual life is more or less to declare war against material energy. The material energy is trying to entrap the conditioned soul as much as possible, and when conditioned soul tries to get out of her clutches by spiritual advancement of knowledge, material nature becomes more stringent and vigorous in her efforts to test how much the aspiring spiritualist is sincere. The material energy or Maya/illusion wills the offer with more allurements.

******

Failure is the pillar of success. In the spiritual life especially, failure is not discouraging.

******

A person, who has approached Krishna, is better situated/ positioned, even though he may fall down from the yogic platform.

******

A man either serves illusion or reality. The constitutional position of living identity is like to be a servant, not a master. One is apparently a servant to his wife, of his children and of his business/ work. Furthermore, when one comes to the platform of knowledge, he understands that in all circumstances he is servant only.

******

No relationship in this material world is actual or eternal. We must always remember that these ephemeral relationships we have are simply perverted reflections of that eternal relationship, we have with the supreme personality of Godhead. Relations of child, master, wife, husband, friend etc. are simply reflections of that relationship we have with God.

******

One, who sticks to a particular point and does not make further progress is called by the particular name i.e. Karma yogi, Jnana Yogi, Raja Yogi etc., but if one is fortunate enough to come to the point of Bhakti Yoga, then the Krishna Consciousness develops in him, which is to be understood that he has surpassed all the Yoga systems.

******

8

Science of Consciousness

Interesting enough, when scientists/common men fail again and again in their attempts to achieve their goal, they pray consciously or unconsciously to Almighty/God for help. Does this not indicate the existence of supreme scientist/power/super human being?

******

Apple from tree does not fall while green but only falls while it is ripe. Newton's law of Gravitation fails to explain this natural phenomenon.

******

Wealth, Strength, Knowledge, Beauty, Fame and Renunciation etc.; for all these the expansion of Almighty/God have His eternal Abode.

******

Every thing is there and nothing can come out of nothing. If someone claims that any thing is belonged to him, he is totally ignorant of Supreme Power of God.

******

As per Plank, entropy of perfect crystal at absolute zero degree is equal to zero. Factually, there is no means available for measuring directly the absolute entropies. Therefore the proof of this law is beyond the realm of experimental science.

******

The birth, disease, old age and death are the signals of the changing of physical body.

******

As per Darwin species had not been independently created but had descended; like varieties from other species. If this theory is correct, it is surprising, why can't we see the intermediate forms of species as connecting links?

******

As per Vedas Men, Animals, beasts, Birds etc., all species are created simultaneously; because whatever desires the living entities had at the last annihilation, are again manifested.

******

One attains the human form of life after transmigrating through 84 lakhs species of life by the process of gradual evolution.

******

There are 90 Lakhs species of aquatic life, 20 Lakhs species of plants and trees, 11 Lakhs species of insects, 10 Lakhs species of bird life, 30 Lakhs species of beasts and 4 Lakhs species/ grades of human beings of different levels of consciousness.

******

Purpose of education is to solve the problem of life. But it only increases sense gratification more and more, thereby creating more and more paths of degradation.

******

Lower forms of life such as animals, birds and plants do not suffer from sinful activities because they never violate the laws of nature. The body of animals is developed and meant in a way, they are supposed to act for their livelihood. However, when spirit/soul comes to the level of a human being, the living entity is then subjected to the results of his actions i.e. Karma-phala/ action and reactions.

******

Whoever, at the time of death, quits his body, remembering the name of the Lord consciously, he attains Him.

******

By the mercy of Almighty, one gets a spiritual master, and by the mercy of spiritual master, one approaches to Almighty.

******

The absolute truth must descend from the absolute platform. It is not to be understood by ascending process. Without sacrifice, one cannot live happy on this planet and not one can achieve something substantial in this life.

******

There is no difference between the holy name of the Lord and Lord Himself. One can chant the holy name of the Lord consciously in a humble state of mind and be more modest than even a tree.

******

9

Spiritual Practices

Moral life, aesthetic sense, hunger for knowledge, truth, and activity are the saving and ennobling elements in a man's life.

******

In the primary stages, when the animal instinct is strong in man, religion for him can only be submission to sacred beliefs and observance of, for forms and ceremonies only.

******

Art, morality, search for knowledge, intense activity, clarity and love help immensely in training the mind to feel and perceive finely.

******

Some times intense activity satisfies and eventually destroys the worldly instincts, and gives us the taste of a higher and finer life.

******

Pranayama, singing of divine name and glory, His praise, without mental preparation have danger that this may evoke too much emotion, which drags the mind down to dangerously low levels.

******

Morality, art and knowledge are the only way for higher life. And our food, environment, climate, illness etc., all these have influence on our mind.

******

Certain part of the mind is always in close association with body. Any change in body produces the desired changes in mind; and vice versa changes in mind and thinking affect the human body.

******

Harmonious development of head, heart and hand i.e. thinking, emotions and physical activity are required for spiritual progress.

******

Spirituality is concerned with perception where as intellect is concerned with development of things.

******

Mind is to be annihilated to reach Almighty. So long as the mind remains, real knowledge of Almighty is impossible; one has to go beyond this. The paradox is, where there is no mind, how can there be world!

******

What is Spirituality? It is complete cessation of Vritties/mental tendencies. The universe, subjective speaking, is nothing but an aggregate of Virrities/mental tendencies. Spiritual progress consists in reducing the number of these tendencies, until the tendencies relating to God alone remains in mind. When the material's Vritties/ tendencies come, God's Vritties/tendencies vanish. Both cannot stay and move together.

******

Occult powers have nothing to do with spirituality.

******

Constant struggle with mind leads to neurosis. This is dangerous, it must be avoided.

******

A householder can never practice universal love. The very mode of his life is a contradiction. He has to submit to powers of others at time against his consciousness. The Sannyasi has an opportunity to realize it.

******

Although consciously we want to realize God, our mind often has other secret desires, which distract and divide us; of course, if we can formally renounce the world; we can avoid many of these distractions.

******

Unless a man is inspired by spiritual ideals, it is extremely difficult, nay impossible, to keep the sexual instinct in check.

******

From the higher standpoint of one, who is seeking to realize God, it is far short of the whole duty of man.

******

If we are to neutralize the effect of worldly influences, we must assiduously practice every minute of our waking life; what is called spirituality.

******

Love relation of a family is only Maya/illusion.

******

Unselfish acts, worship, purification of mind lead to Karma Yoga; and God absorption comes by it self without any force.

******

Wherever the mind is, the energy and blood are concentrated.

******

Sexual abstention is absolutely necessary for spiritual progress. Since higher spiritual practices causes a great strain on the nerves system and brain, which are impaired by incontinence; these become too weak to bear that great strain. With spiritual progress, sexual desire diminishes automatically.

******

An excess of acid, mostly causes fatigue, in the physical system.

******

It is a good and very beneficial practice to observe partial or complete fast on the day after a nocturnal emission, praying and thinking of God. This has a wonderful counter effect.

******

The way to God is beset with all possible obstacles. Only an adamantine resolve can overcome them.

******

10

From Yoga

One is the force of life by which you live and move. And other is the force of mind by which you think and know.

******

The Absolute, which is beyond time and space, is infinite. And that, which is relative to time and space is limited, is finite. The state of mind is not absolute. But, with the concentrated mind, one keeps on following the path of light.

******

Sometimes the food is not digested due to the lack of acidity; however, some acidity in the system is also required.

******

During Sirs-asana and Kumbak i.e. retention of breathe, consumption of oxygen decreases but the rate of oxygen assimilation increases.

******

Diseases such as Cancer are born out of mind but manifested in the body over a long period of time. Any disease may be from mind or from body; any thing that happens to the body affects the mind and anything, which affects the mind, effects the body.

******

For the spiritualized body, the nutrition is created internally that keeps the body fit and healthy.

******

Many diseases originate in the mind and travel into the body. They are known as psyche-somatic diseases. When diseases originates in the body and travel into the mind, they are known as Somatic-psychic diseases.

******

If there is improper distribution of prana from Manipura Chakra to the Adrenal glands, one suffers from fear-psychosis, colitis and other Somatic diseases.

******

When Pranic energy is duly converted into magnetic energy, it can be transmitted outside of the body through fingers, a look, or a thought.

******

Locations of Various Chakras in body are as follows:

Mooladhaha at Perineum; Swadhisthana at coccyx; Manipura behind the Navel; Anahata behind the Sternum; Vishudhi behind the throat pit; Ajna at the Pineal Gland and right at the top of spinal cord in the Medulla Oblongata.

******

Man is a composition of three basic forces i.e. Paraná, Mental and Spiritual. Both prana and mental forces are type of physical forces. Meditation helps to climb the spiritual force/energy created in the system directly to the Sahasrara Chakra.

******

For a strong man, every ascent is a joy and every descent is a game.

******

Mental tension can be avoided by more physical Karma yoga.

******

One learns gradually that spiritual life virtually dehypnotizes him with time.

******

The evolution of life that one has reached in human incarnation has never moved in one straight line. It has moved back and forth through out the life span. This is how the energy flows.

******

Distractions are born out of desires; of ignorance and unawareness of spirit; when one is not following the inner path side by side with external life; he will have more distractions.

******

Unless one is able to transcend the mind and body, distractions will not leave him.

******

11

Spiritual Experiences

Maya is a cosmic illusion and Avidya is an individual ignorance.

******

When we are inadequate in ourselves but our ego is strong, we tend to blame others.

******

Do not be attached to the pleasures received from the objects of the world. Treat them as means for spiritual progress.

******

The strongest is he, who walks all alone.

******

Latent desires manifest during meditation.

******

The more you know, the more you decide to learn. When you have sharpened the faculty of discrimination, you firmly treat your path without any doubts.

******

It is not necessary to renounce any thing. Only the sense of possessiveness should be renounced.

******

In the path of action, duties are not renounced, but are performed skillfully and selflessly.

******

Gandhi ji lived and and walked as if his soul is out of his body. He was very clear that the poverty in India is not because of spirituality but because of not practicing spirituality, and not knowing the technique of integrating spirituality with external life.

******

Voice of silence is supreme. It is above all communications and all levels of consciousness.

******

Hatred and worry are negative habits that control the mind. Meditation and contemplation expand the mind.

******

As Shiva Lingam is for Indians, the Star of David's is for Jewels.

******

Seven Systems of Indian Philosophy is:

1. Vedanta;
2. Yoga;
3. Samkhya i.e. Purusha and Prakiriti;
4. Vaisheshika that discusses earth, water, fire, air, space, Time, mind, soul and their mutual relationship;
5. Mimamsa i.e. salvation through action;
6. Nyaya i.e. Logician school;
7. and Buddhism.

******

Happiness does not come merely through human endeavor but comes through grace.

******

To learn more about man's inner life rhythms, one should learn to go beyond desire and cultivate the inward sensitivity and one-pointedness of that mind, which can seek help from finer forces of rhythmic vibrations.

******

12

Qualities Worth Having

Constant struggling to be good, daily prayers for wisdom and listening to the voice of God within you shall bring the real wisdom.

******

Qualities worth having are:

1. A sense of wonder;
2. The art of conversation;
3. Patience;
4. Preserve;
5. Silence;
6. How to take sickness;
7. How to live with difficult people;
8. Generosity;
9. Being a gentleman;
10. Adaptability;
11. Justice;
12. Appreciation of beauty;
13. Love;
14. Unselfishness;
15. Prayer;
16. Contentment;
17. Gratitude;
18. The sweetest virtue;
19. Love of reading;

20. Desire for knowledge;
21. Keeping fit;
22. Religious;
23. Courage;
24. How to take pain;
25. Readiness for death;
26. Self control;
27. A proper understanding of sex;
28. How to be chaste;
29. Self denial-Mortification-Tapasya/Penance;
30. Tolerance;
31. Sympathy;
32. How to meet a crisis;
33. Ability to enjoy work;
34. A proper understanding of money;
35. Good friends;
36. Advice;
37. Ability to take future;
38. How to take success;
39. How to accept and use one's defects;
40. Not judging others;
41. To see one's usefulness;
42. The habit of thinking;
43. Getting the best out of the imagination;
44. How to study;
45. To use time well;
46. Culture;
47. Ambition;
48. Concentration on the present;
49. Awareness of the presence of God;
50. Peace;
51. Wisdom;
52. The Spirit of God.

******

13

Beyond Words

It is the very being; it is the essence of all words; see and relate beyond words; then there is no lie in your life. If you manipulate words; it is lie; if you play on words; it is joke; if you rely on words; it is ignorance; if you transcend words; it is wisdom.

******

Earlier people think in terms of Ethiopia i.e. Satya Yuga, but now people think in terms of Dystopia i.e. fear, gloomy and oldosem. World is going through destruction. It cannot improve any more.

******

World has already achieved degage, height of bravery, education, rationality. It has much less to achieve further in this direction. But it has created ecological crisis, energy crisis, nuclear crisis and population explosion.

******

The dilemma before persons are; How to die? It is a philosophical question, since man is living on borrowed time.

******

Buddha, Aristotle period, and earliest discoveries of science started more or less in the same time, but science has made unbounded progress. However, religion has not produced a single Buddha. The reason being that the man's mind has tendencies of crocodile and horse brain, which govern the lust and anger of human mind. That is the reason with the evolution, activities of crocodile and horse brain drastically increased because of more indulgence in lust and consequently to anger.

******

Human mind has reached its "crisis" limit. Now it has to evolutes consciously i.e. evolution to super-consciousness state has to take place.

******

Basically Yoga is nothing but psychological discipline i.e. rising of consciousness and disappearance of ego.

******

Thinking is one of the greatest joys of human mind.

******

He who cans "does"; and he who cannot, "teaches".

******

With rational knowledge, one is tune with the scientific man; with intuitive knowledge added, one is tune with the total man; with no knowledge added, one is in tune with nature.

******

Each person has to fight his own battle of Kurukshetra. It is as a war, however, not only worth winning; but for maintaining the divine order of the universe and of the eternal relationship between the soul and God; this war sooner or later is required to win.

******

The birth of knowledge and birth of love are not two different events. The moment, we have the knowledge of the omnipresent Lord; the same instant love for Him springs in our heart.

******

Four impediments in particular are responsible for diminishing one's natural taste for the holy name:

1. Ignorance of eternal principles;
2. Frailties of heart;
3. Evil propensities;
4. Offences.

******

Devotion and Reflection are independent as religion and philosophy. Religion without philosophy is sentiment, or sometime fanaticism, while philosophy without religion is mental speculation.

******

Materialism should be avoided at the Burial ground, near the patient, at temple, and near Guru.

******

If you are looking for perfection, then you are not at the source of joy. Underneath the world, there is perfection. But world appears imperfect. Only imperfections show; Perfection hides.

******

Devotion shown to God always evokes some form of plain or mysterious response. God ignores no true devotee. It is He, who is Chintamani, 'the jewel that grants every thing and fulfills all desires".

******

One should seek God first; last and all the time; not for His gifts; but as one's ultimate aim. Then he will find, in the abundance of God's love, all and every thing for which he longs.

******

Truth has no direction, no goal. Truth itself is the goal: truth is infinite. Feeling and experience are infinity with in this finite body; living timeless within the time span of life is the goal; uncovering bliss within the misery is the ultimate.

******

When you are happy; mind expands; and then time appears short. When you are unhappy; time appears too long. When the mind has equanimity; you transcend time.

******

Samadhi is a state of mindlessness and timelessness.

******

Virtues in general cannot be cultivated. A seeker should know that he is borne with virtues, otherwise he cannot be seeker. When you recognize the virtues in others, it shows that you have those virtues present in seed form, and you must nurture them.

******

14

Love

Love is a fluid, it cannot break. It makes you weak. When a bud breaks, it becomes a flower. It breaks for the good. A flower cannot break. Similarly, when heart breaks it becomes divine. In true love, there is no heartbreak. A broken heart means broken demands, broken expectations and broken hopes.

******

Beyond the event is knowledge; beyond a person is love; beyond the object is infinity. Knowledge is not an event; it is beyond event.

******

When you love your personality, you become love. If you cannot love yourself, you cannot find yourself. Behind every object is infinity.

******

Where there is authority, there cannot be love. Where there is love, there is no authority. With a true friend, you share your happy moment; your sorrows; it is nothing but heart to heart love.

******

In true sense, when you love some one, you listen to him, you observe him/her closely, and when you really starting to like, you will like to venture and finally you will evolve with the beloved and merge in each other. So, "L" for word "love" is listening; "O" is for observation; "V" of word love is for venture; and "E" is for evolvement together for the ultimate mergence and knowledge.

******

The world does not care how you are inside. It only looks to your outside behavior. The divine does not care how you are outside; it only cares for your inner core. Never one should carve house of tiny bit of dislike in your heart. It should always be fresh, soft, and full of love and emit a fragrance like a rose. Be in touch with source and make life a celebration every moment.

******

Whatever you can prove, you can disprove also. God is beyond our proof and disproof. God is an experience.

******

All life moves with intention. Desire is that intention, which turns into a feverish thought in you. Desire brings a disease in the mind and an obsession in due course.

******

Longing/love can come out of gratefulness and gratitude. Longing does not come out of complaint or frustration, which will bring only anger and hatred.

******

Love, grace and knowledge can cut the bondage for Karmas.

******

No good action is waste in life. In the past, all you have gone through, has built the foundation and has brought the walls up. Now at this stage, you are here to put on the roof, to complete it. Nothing is waste; all positive efforts bring the fruits sooner or later.

******

One is always connected with God and not separates from Him. Wave cannot be without ocean and not the fish without water; it may be in deep; inside; on the surface; but not without water.

******

If you take something from circle, the circle is not complete. The completeness comes because it is total.

******

Devotion brings faith, compassion, and responsibility, which in turns give knowledge, wisdom and love. Real devotion means being with divine.

******

Through understanding and observation, health can be retained. Pure consciousness is pure love and love is highest healing on the earth.

******

Love is not just emotion. It is existence. It is what you are made of. To know this, you must be free of fear and anxiety. Only with love system is purified.

******

Health in Sanskrit means stabilized in self and love. Health means being centered. When mind is free from anger; guilt; it is centered. Then only it can heal by itself. You can become like ocean and nothing will disturb you and not even big mountain like miseries. You will have perfect peace.

******

When fear comes, a sensation arises in the chest region. One must observe this sensation and go deep into this. Like fear other emotions in the mind creates a corresponding sensation in the body. When you observe, these sensations disappear. These are released and mind becomes clear, peaceful and full of love.

******

When some one is pained and troubled, he does not want to come back under same conditions/situations of love. If the conditions were wonderful and full of love and divinity, then the intrinsic desire not to come back would drop naturally.

******

Love does not cause pain. A love grows and stands forever under all conditions. In innermost core one is always full of love; he wants love only. And true knowledge is just to develop the innermost sensitive core.

******

Ego really obstructs us from the innocent love. It is like a dream. A dream exists until it does not exit/disappear.

******

A seed has covering or shell. On soaking it in water, covering will vanish/disappear like an ego to make us natural and full of love as we are innocently born. Also, when knowledge is full; the ego drops automatically; and simplicity is drawn.

******

15

Deep Thoughts

Illusion is the error of perception and knowing illusion, as illusion, is knowledge.

******

Every experience leaves a residue that clouds the intellect.

******

You can be at ease with uncertainty of the world when you realize the certainty of the consciousness. Often people are certain about the world and uncertain about God. They rely, which is not reliable and get upset. Uncertainty causes craving for stability but we forget that most stable thing in universe is the Self.

******

If one is certain and is able to perceive that every thing in the world is uncertain, then he is liberated.

******

Often people think that certainty is freedom. But if some one feels freedom when he is not certain, then that is the real freedom.

******

Generally, certainty or uncertainty is relative. Being certain about the uncertainty makes us certain about the existence of the Absolute; and this brings a certain faith in our deep contemplation about the Absolute.

******

Playing/acting in uncertainty makes life a game, a challenge. Uncertainty about matter brings certainty about consciousness. Uncertainty about self creates fear.

******

When you are ahead of time, world drags you back. And when time is ahead of you, then you are surprised and shocked.

******

Even a few moments of Samadhi infuses the mind with energy. Moments of twilight of consciousness, experiences the timelessness that gives the nectar of blissful state.

******

Life is a combination of form and formless when merged in Self. Similarly feelings have no form but their expressions have form. The Self has no form but their abode has form. Wisdom and grace have no form but are expressed through form only. Discarding the formless, one moves out from source/origin of the knowledge. Discarding the farm one becomes a dreamer, a lost ascetic or emotionally unbalanced. Form and formless are manifested and un-manifested states of the Almighty that move the human life cycle.

******

Formality improves communication, and cordiality improves communion and oneness. Formality and communication exist with duality, but love and knowledge are based on cordiality. However, organization cannot function when formality is abandoned.

******

Cordiality is the core of one's existence; formality is the outer shell. When outer shell is thin, it can reflect inner light. For smooth going, we must maintain balance between formality and cordiality.

******

In respect and surrender, the head bends and try to touch/ meet the heart. The head that is stiff because of egoism will have to bend sooner or later, either in surrender or shame. Shame brings guilt but shyness adds to beauty.

******

There is no independent existence for anyone, so in fact there is nothing to surrender. One must go through surrender absolutely to realize that it is not more than an illusion.

******

One, who is irresponsible, cannot surrender since he is lazy and/ or fearful or both. In fact total responsibility is complete surrender.

******

Surrender eventually leads you to self-reliance because there is nothing else than the Self.

******

One, who is surrendered to knowledge, is committed to sharing with others. To surrender is the foundation of responsibility.

******

Limited responsibility may make you tired. But unlimited responsibility empowers you and bring you joy.

******

An uncommitted mind is miserable. A committed mind may at times experience rough weather but it will reap fruit in due course. When you make service as your sole purpose in life; it eliminates fear; focuses your mind and gives you meaning.

******

Richest of all are those, who share themselves. A person's wealth is measured by his ability to share and not by what he holds.

******

Any one, who runs after success or who claims to be successful reveals his limitation; If he feels very successful; it means that he has underestimated himself. In fact taking pride in any achievement is belittling one self.

******

Work does not tire you as much as does the sense of doer-ship.

******

It is wonderful to know that all of your talents are for others. Your good voice is for others to hear. If you are a good cook, it is for other to eat. If you write a book, it is for others to read. If you are good surgeon, it is to heal others. If you are not making you of/as your talents, the talents will not come to you by God's grace.

******

Service without attitude; love without reason; knowledge without intellect i.e. wisdom; life beyond time and events; is what you are. The more you give, the more strength will be given to you.

******

A person, who knows that he owns God, is not in hurry for any thing. Infinite patience arises/develops in him. Patience in mind and dynamism in action are right virtues, which cops up in him.

******

God does not test an individual since He knows. Only one needs to test him self.

******

Most of the rituals and prayers are just attempts to trick the divine. They are without any devotion. God is the very core of human existence. God clings to you like a baby. Penance, prayers etc. are His nourishments.

******

Every one of us is chariot, carrying power of God within i.e. soul.

******

One must be deeply sincere in his attempts to get God's Blessings. Without His Bliss, joy in the world is impermanent.

******

One's body belongs to world and spirit/soul belongs to divine. One must have firm faith in God's divine name and then move on to silence and have faith on abode of silence. This will bring perfection in him. Divinity is only security; and he must keep money, family and friends where they are.

******

In science, knowledge comes first then faith follows. In spirituality, faith comes first and then knowledge follows. Meditation pours knowledge of consciousness. Faith only brings stability, calmness, love and divine Blessings. Faith resolves all the queries.

******

Forgetfulness of the infinity is misery.

******

It is strange to observe and analyze that God is not a good economist. Look at the tree, shedding leaves and getting new one. Almighty takes experienced old people away and child is born and with time; he is also taken away after that he gets experience. Is it not economical if God could have given hundred more years to Einstein to use his caliber?

******

If we feel high and next moment we feel low and if it continued with this feeling continuously, soon we will be ruined. We must feel like water; do not be stiff; stiffness is like ego; water can take any shape; it makes ripples with slightest shaking; we must have discriminative acceptance attitude to be happy in life.

******

Be on low level and humble like ocean. Ocean becomes great because it has accepted to be lowest without any egoism. Can any source be deeper and lower than ocean? It is wonderful to imagine and perceive that water in ocean does not remain always there. Heat of sun transforms it as clouds; go up the sky and rain.

******

16

Self Knowledge–The Best Companion

When you are miserable, know that you have gone away from the Self.

******

When you realize that everyone is a part of yourself, you enjoy the whole world without a sense of craving.

******

Share your joy with every one but your problems with the Self, the Almighty only.

******

Either through knowledge or through problems and miseries, you ultimately come to the point that there is nothing, nothing and nothing. Even if you accept the one iota of this, the changes start happening.

******

Intuition, discovery and knowledge go beyond rational mind. Rational mind is like rail/road track that is fixed in grooves. Truth is beyond it. However, irrational mind is free, and just acts.

******

Freedom and discipline are opposite on surface, but complementary to each other. Knowledge is both freedom and discipline. Freedom without discipline is an absolute misery and discipline without freedom is suffocating.

******

Orderliness becomes monotonous in due course, but chaos is always stressful.

******

Perfect balance can only be maintained by staying with the Self only. It gives peace, calmness and intuitive knowledge.

******

Diksha is nothing but to get direction to proceed to the realm of the being from the Self-realized master. It is the journey with heart to heart communication.

******

In spirituality Sama is equanimity of inner life i.e. to behave in the same way both in good and bad situations/conditions, and Dana is giving/donating and forgiving with discrimination.

******

There are four doubts in life, which every body experiences some time or the other i.e. doubt on self; doubt on the technique; doubt on the experience; and finally the doubt on the success.

******

What so ever you internally experience with other person on close association with him, basically you are seeing in you self.

******

Without love, surrender and devotion, meditation will be just mechanical and dry, and will not fetch any thing.

******

One must not force the mind; let it go where he wants. Follow the mind and bring it back to the proper thought, and then try to become thought less and enter into the realm of silence. This only will bring you near the Almighty.

******

When senses are with the self then only happiness is experienced. Away from self bring the sorrow and misery. Self is not mutable; not changes; it is permanent.

******

Mind has to be totally empty to get the feel and presence of Almighty/Master. No mental relation should be made to have His glimpses; mind must be in absolute silent state with nothingness in it.

******

Whenever happiness has disappeared from your life, look deep within you and you will see/feel that it is because of desire. Desire is the cause of misery. Desire is illusion—the Maya. It arises with pleasant experience or existing vacuumed in life or with past impressions.

******

Fortunate are those who don't have desire because there is fulfillment needed before the desires arise. Somewhat fortunate are those whose desires fulfill immediately, and those are less fortunate who take lot of time for fulfillment or never get fulfilled. If you don't desire, you will not get pleasure out of it even after you get every thing. However, he is the king and very near to God who does not have any desire.

******

When you desire truth, desires drop off. Desire for truth remove all other desires. Desires/ intentions separate you from God. One must offer all his desires to God, and then he becomes divine. He is Jeewan Mukta: the liberated; lacking and needing nothing in life.

******

17

Truth, Radiance and Divinity

"Ra" in Sanskrit means, which is radiant and "Ma" means myself. So, "Rama" is what shines within us. That which is radiant in every particle is "Rama".

******

Dashratha means the "Ten Charioted One". This signifies five sense organs and five organs of action. Kaushalya means "skilled". This signifies that when five senses and five organs of action are skillfully used, radiance i.e. Rama appears/is born. And when these ten organs are co-operating with each other, awareness/ consciousness as Laksha (Lakshman) is born with this divine radiance to Sumitra as brother and "Good friend" of Rama.

******

Inside infinite divine qualities of love, beauty and compassion do not show up fully outside, which is finite with faults and imitations. Inside lodged knowledge as wisdom is not easily understood by others; and divine light is never perceived by external vision.

******

If you are dispassionate, blessings are poured to you as knowledge of the Self. If you are self less and hard working, blessings will come to you as happiness.

******

When one realizes the futility of the words, then only he perceives/knows that his life is going deeper.

******

It is wonderful to treat God as child and then you will not have any demand from Him. You will only try to give Him love and all the best things, you have; and in return what you will get in abundance, only you can perceive and no body else. God clings to you like a child. He needs you to nourish Him with Sadhana, Sat sang and Seva. God has infinite qualities and forms. When you accept Him with so much varieties of divinity, you cease to be fanatics or a fundamentalist.

******

We live in words and think about words, bothered about words. There is no rest from words in our life. Words are root cause of worries. There is no worry without words. Our happiness/ unhappiness depends on words spoken by others. Life is indeed is very shallow if we base it on words. Anything that is very profound in life, deep or meaningful, cannot be expressed in words including experience of love and gratitude. Real beauty and true friendship has no words. The day we realize that words are incompetent, we can realize that we gained depth in our life, and we are deeper into existence. Being in deep silent stage, we can easily visualize all this from the deep core of our heart.

******

If we go deeper, we can find that there is a divine music all the time in our bodies and we are not aware of all this. Divinity has to be planted like roses in our life, and then divine melody can be enjoyed but grass like Vasanas grow by it self and no plantation is required; instead these need to be removed from time to time.

******

When one perceives the real beauty, some unusual things happens in the core of his heart as if some life energy, which was blocked, just opens up, like a spring opens up. He starts worshiping the beauty and surrenders to it. If he does not surrender to this divine beauty; but he wants to posses it; how can he possess some thing unique and much greater to him? He can only admire and worship the divine beauty, which is always young and graceful.

******

Only that which is temporary, small or perishable needs protection while which is permanent, big or vast does not. Protection prevents transformation and it cannot happen in a state of total protection. Protection is always limited to time, and to perishable things. Truth, peace and happiness do not need protection because they are not temporary. Body and mind need protection but not the self and soul. The purpose of body and mind is to create a world of divinity around.

******

Music stimulates ears; sight stimulates eyes; Sadana and Satsanga stimulate the soul and this takes to the silence; silence is "Self" or very close to Self; Silence is a "soul". More one is mentally "Silent"; the more one is near to the Almighty.

******

When the intellect discusses the mundane things, it starts dividing existence. And when it discusses, wisdom and truth then only it unites. It brings forth the transcendental. Only then wisdom, divinity and truth flow through the intellect.

******

Fine factors that influence mind are place, time, and food, past impressions, association and actions. Furthermore, awareness, alertness, knowledge and meditation help to erase the past impressions.

******

Desire, action and awareness of the Self are the manifestation of the divine energy. When desires dominate, Self-awareness will be at its lowest level resulting in stress and sorrow. When action dominates; restlessness and disease are the net out come/result. However, when awareness dominates, happiness is drawn; and when desire and action are directed to the divinity, Self-knowledge is attained.

******

Being in bitter in love experience and yet being undisturbed; caring yet not worried; persistent yet not perturbed; are the obvious sign of shining within.

******

The six distortions that do not exist in the Self are: expansion; contraction; evolution; decay; beginning-Anaadi; and lack of Abahava.

******

All the experiences are on the circumference and they are continuously changing. The one, who experiences, is at the centre; it is the Self.

******

Some questions can only be answered in Silence. Silence is the goal of all answers. Thoughts are not the goal of life. Goal is silence. The easy way to silence thoughts is to arouse feeling. Through feeling peace, joy and love are drawn. Silence discloses an answer "Who am I?" In life only Silence of mind is "complete" to resolve all queries.

******

All the events that have happened are just fall in place for you to be where you are just now. Entire phenomenal world is happening on its own. You have only to watch and witness.

******

You never know from where the thoughts arise. Thinking is the cause of worry. You can only think what you know. Basically, when you know, then what is the need of thinking about it? It is surprising that more you are drawn to think positively; you move and are drawn towards negatively.

******

You don't need to think positively; nor need you to think negative. You have to transcend the thinking; understand the thinking. Thinking is like a cloud in thy space. It comes and goes. Watch and observe, you will find yourself in another plane of existence. This is the truth of life and this is nothing but freedom.

******

18

A Complete Trust

Your family, people around you, you cannot trust. Sometimes your own senses can deceive you. People change statements in no time. Basically, you cannot trust any thing. Either you go to for total trust and trust every thing or trust nothing. Finally, it leads to the same point and you will be uncertain all the time to make up your mind.

******

Sorrow cannot stay; if you are on the path of self-realization; you become trust worthy. To help others become your internal nature and habit; at times it may be at the cost of your self.

******

If you don't get what you desire. Have a complete trust that God wants some thing else for you. This may be much favorable to you.

******

Have a trust that God always keeps you under control by giving you suitable problems to keep you in right track and under peace; otherwise you will become head strong with time and lose control with your self - centre.

******

Waves cannot be without water so you being in this world cannot be without God. Trust in God will make you strong in all walks of life.

******

It is matter of trust that south facing gives respect/honor; west facing gives wealth; east facing gives long life; and north facing gives peace of mind. Seeing dirty mirror is not healthy. Also, while sleeping to put head in direction of south or east is good for health and sound sleep.

******

If you fight with your feelings, they take longer time to get dissolve. The best way is to "Let go" and "Surrender". Surrender means having trust in love. Every night you surrender your body, and go to sleep. Morning you come back; and this makes you happy; relax and peaceful.

******

19

Silence—The Mode of Deep Knowledge

Almighty is the junction of the presence; and the present is without duality. Whenever every cell, every atom of mind and body get totally immersed in the presence and in the present, one experiences something ecstatic; something beyond this world; and something beyond existence. And finally experience of eternity comes in the realm of silence.

******

God is the totality. Everything is God. There is nothing that can be outside God. Whether good or evil, both exist in God. One cannot be separate from God. One can never be away from space/ God; whatsoever one does. God is omnipresent. The only difference is that one knows it; another one does not know.

******

In silence there is no duality. This is just a taste of being; all by oneself. But one has to go deeper in silence and his mind should be there in silence. One's mind should be conscious and aware of his body. When some one is with body and mind in silence, he is with God. Where there is mind, there is inner energy. And this is the secret of being healthy and to cure the diseases appearing in the body.

******

Silence is expansion, and expansion of awareness is presence. In deep silence, the presence is enormous and limitless.

******

Surprising, one can never meet God. When he meets God, he disappears, only God remains. This path of existence is so narrow that two cannot exist. Either he is there or the God is there. Even, when there is awareness/consciousness, there is no God. Maya/illusion and God cannot exist together, as light and darkness cannot be together.

******

You cannot measure depth of water with a stick made of salt. The moment it touches the water, it dissolves. Similarly, you are dissolved as you merge in God. So, in your true nature; you are God; free of guilt; silent; and full of surrender. This has to be realized. This is the ultimate goal of life.

******

The followings must be understood as:

Prakrti/Purusha as (Maya, illusion, senses)/self;

Ksetra/Ksetrajna is as (body, gross)/ (Subtle/Casual); and

Jnana/Jneya is as knowledge/known.

******

The matter after union with spirit becomes functional and alive.

******

The path of Self-realization begins with action, passes through knowledge in silence and ends in meditation. Brahman/God cannot be understood by mind/intellect. One can only merge in it in deep silence. Since if God is there then there will be no one else.

******

Through articulate (divine sound vibrations i.e. mantra) and then by in articulation (through deep silent intuitive mind), Almighty can be realized.

******

There are 24 items come under Ksetra as per Indian Spiritual Science i.e. Space, Air, Water, Fire, Earth, and Eyes, Nose, Ear, Tongue, Skin, as well as Feet, Hands, Tongue, Reproduction organs, Excrete organs along with 5 senses and Mind, Intellect, Ego and Vasanas.

******

There are five material values in the world i.e. Wealth, Name, Fame, Power and Status.

******

There are five changes in human life as he is born i.e. Birth, Growth, Decay, Disease and Death.

******

One needs to transcend body, mind and intellect to merge with the cosmic power.

******

Only weak people seek company. They cannot live alone. Being alone they feel loneliness.

******

Jnani/knowledgeable is self- sufficient, self -poised and self-pleased. Those, who lack self-sufficiency, they feel/compelled to socialize and meet people.

******

Self-realization exhausts all vasanas.

******

Brahman/Almighty is neither SAT nor ASAT. He is Omni present and is not movable.

******

Brahman/Almighty enlivens the qualities. It is flow of current (Self). As developed the Gunas/qualities; accordingly the person will act.

******

The un-manifested Brahman never moves while the manifested Brahman moves, just as electricity do not move but it moves a motor/drive.

******

Brahman is pure consciousness. The un-manifested Brahman is one, while its manifestations are multi billions and multi dimensions. Brahman is omnipresent so immovable.

******

Cause and effect are like chicken and egg relation; as well as they have tree and seed relations.

******

When Purusha's spirit functions through Prakriti, it becomes an individual Jiva. And Ataman acts like a fuel in Jiva. Ataman/soul does every thing still perform nothing.

******

Rational person is a developed intellectual; while emotional person is completely devotional.

******

God does not do. God/Self/ Electricity is a flow, and it flows where you want it to flow. It is a force behind everything but does nothing by itself.

******

Self within us is like a wooden piece; remains immaculate/pure; untainted by the world. When we have clinging attachment; self disappears; its force/impact is not felt and then we suffer.

******

There are twenty-six divine qualities, and six demoniac and asurika qualities.

******

Divine qualities are: fearlessness, purity, steadfastness in knowledge and yoga, charity, self-restraint, sacrifice, self study, austerity, uprightness, harmlessness, truth, absence of anger, renunciation, peace, absence of calumny (not demeaning others), compassion, un-covetousness, gentleness, modesty, absence of fickleness, spiritual luster, forgiveness, steadfastness, courage, absence of malice, absence of pride.

******

Demoniac qualities are:

Ostentation: hypocritical behavior; trying simulating virtue;

Arrogance: unjustly:

Self-conceit: exaggerated opinion of one self;

Anger: harshness; and Ignorance.

******

Illusory world cannot exist without real world.

******

If desires exceed wealth, one becomes poor.

******

The law of life is that you are always punished by your reaction and not for your actions in general.

******

The cause of mental suffering lies in the neglect of self within.

******

Way to hell is broadly: desire; greed; and anger. On the contrary, the way to success is devotion; determination; and drive.

******

During birth only physical body is developed where as mental-intellect are in embryonic state. How they develop later, it is mystery.

******

Austerity (Tapa) of mind is:

Serenity; Gentleness; Silence; Self-restraint; and Pure disposition.

******

Rajsika works for Reverence (Satkar), Worship, Honor and Ostentation (hypocritical austerity)

******

The way to gain anything is to lose it.

******

Sanyasa is renunciation of egocentric desire by dedicating action to the supreme goal of Self-realization.

******

Renunciation is the growth of personality

******

Dropping of anxiety brings peace of mind as well as success in action.

******

Renunciation functions as cause, Sanyasa as effect. Renunciation suggests mode of action while Sanyasa is a result.

******

Sattvika sees unity in diversity where as Rajsika sees diversity in unity and Tamasika clings to past only.

******

Devotional seeker goes for form worship of Lord and intellectual seeker worships Lord as formless in silence mode and conceives Him as omnipresent divine cosmic energy.

******

The transcendental reality cannot be perceived, felt or conceived. It remains beyond the reach of body, mind and intellect since it is un-manifested.

******

In the final state of meditation, the chant is reduced to mental whisper and it is merged in silence. Absolute silence is the state when one is immerged totally in glory of God. It is the highest achievement.

******

Lord Krishna advises to work for His sake and donate/give the fruits of work to Him.

******

Knowledge, practice, meditation, renunciation of fruits of action and peace are the ascending order to climb the ladder to divinity.

******

You love children, when you direct the same emotional love towards a higher being, it becomes devotion. Devotion of a devotee has no sense of like and dislike. He is aware of his impurity and purity.

******

Everybody expresses his inherent nature. As tiger shows his nature and goat her own.

******

The higher the ideal in life, greater will be potency and peace in action.

******

Studying scriptures can reduce the desires and turn you introvert. There after you will have to plunge into deep meditation to reach the Supreme to become one with God. Ornaments on the body symbolize peace and happiness. Where as weapons signify war and sorrow.

******

The base of the palm and five fingers represents Atman/soul and five sheaths i.e. annamaya, pranamaya, manmaya, and vijnanmaya and anandmaya koshas. Joining palms indicate unifying realities in all. That is the Namaskara.

******

Vishnu has Conch, Chakra, Gadda and Padma (Lotus). The Lotus symbol indicates peace and bliss, The Conch calls for supreme Self. If enemy does not come on right track, He uses Gadda and finally Chakra.

******

Seeing Vishvasaroopa, the layman rejoices; the perfect divine soul bow silently in reverence; and the wicked are terrified.

******

The rope is not the cause for snake. Yet without the rope no snake can emerge from it. Similarly, God remains the underlying reality, the substratum supporting the universe.

******

Matter is short lived. It perishes with time while enlivens spirit persists.

******

A dreamer can only become waked upon waking up. So seeker as dreamer cannot perceive God through body, mind and intellect. He can only merge with God. A seeker must not be in hurry. He must proceed continuously.

******

Those, who work, get attached to it. They may miss ultimate experience, so better be action-less. Otherwise, it is better for work for Almighty only.

******

God is not the object of perception. The seeker gets the knowledge of God by unveiling the Supreme within. In culmination of knowledge, he merges with the Self. He becomes one with the Supreme Being.

******

20

Small Mind, Great Mind and Big Mind

As all rivers merge in ocean. So all small minds merge in big mind. Big mind knows past, present and future. It contains all that you can achieve in this life. Small mind is like waves; it goes on changing statements. Big mind is like an ocean; all discoveries have come from big mind. However, all thoughts come like waves from small mind. Similarly body cells change continuously. In one decade all new cells of body are formed. So constant birth and death of cells continue.

******

When small mind is unaware of big mind, it becomes unstable. The big mind is always in expansion till it become Great mind; the super conscious mind. When small mind becomes silent; it becomes big. When it is quite; one goes into sleep. In absolute silence big mind turns into infinite; cosmic mind i.e. Great mind; which is super conscious.

******

Between God, Guru and Self, there is no difference. Master, an enlightened Guru, is reflecting Big Mind. One must try to merge in Big Self; the Quite Self; ultimately the Silent Self; and turn towards Big Mind and finally in Absolute Silence to be with Great Mind; to Super conscious State.

******

Master is the inner reflection of your own self. When you trust yourself, you trust Master. If you trust Master, then trust in yourself grows.

******

If you cannot love somebody, it shows/means that you cannot love yourself deeply. If you want to achieve this i.e. to love yourself; you start loving Master/God so deeply and then you will see that it does not take you long to turn your small mind into the big mind; and to live in big mind in peace under perfect silent state transforms your big mind into the great mind; and then you will be with the Absolute.

******

If small mind accepts the thoughts then it is called free will or in other words when things happen according to thoughts that come to you, you claim it to be your free will. And when your thoughts were contrary to what happened, you call it destiny. In other scenario if you fight against the thought, it is called destine.

******

In dreams passed impressions of mind are realized. There may be some thoughts of future and intuitions also. In dream either you are in past or day dreaming.

******

Our tongue maintains relation between mind and heart, and it follows which one is dominating.

******

In Mahabharata War Kaurav had 11 Ashohini Sena (5 Sense Organs, 5 Karam Indriya and mind) and 7 Maharathis/great warriors, where as Pandav had 7 Ashohini Sena and 11 Maharathis/ great warriors (reverse that of Kauravas). War lasted for 18 days and Srimad Bhagavad-Gita has 18 Chapters.

******

21

Almighty Never Loses Sight–Have You Always

God is like "Meenakshi" like an eye of a fish. A fish never closes his eyes and always keep watch on younger.

******

Life is a game, a Lila, a play. God does every thing. God wants us just to sit with Him. God says, whatsoever need to be done, I will get it done through you. You just simply stop existing. It is all designed this way. What do you do? Just relax. That is the only thing that you can do. Relax in surrender.

******

If you never had unpleasant moments in life, you would never have pleasant ones either. Then you would never know what pleasantness is. God always takes care and support after giving unpleasantness.

******

Every pinch that you are having in life is for the best, to make your life more lively and enjoyable. This is the law of nature.

******

Being aware of the impermanent nature of our life, the changing nature of happening, one finds that there is something in him that has not changed. This is the reference point by which one can say that things are changing. Getting onto this reference point that is being, which is the source of life, is the real wisdom.

******

A fool is one who is relaxed, who is free, and who is happy. He is not bothered about what he gains whether material, spiritual, or whatsoever. A fool always does some thing and does not get any thing out of it. A fool acts with freedom. If he has not experienced freedom with his act, he cannot be a fool.

******

Life will be fun if you think that "my original home is in heaven, I have come here to rest." To see what is happening around you, and be aware of that. It is a great fun. This is the place of entertainment.

******

One must make his whole life as a game. Game means no purpose. There is nothing. Just take it lightly, easily and play the game. This should be worship and must be celebration.

******

God does every thing and looks after you. If God does not want you to do something, you will never do it. It is impossible to do. The fact that He has allowed you so much freedom to do any thing you like, means, He wants you not to take any thing seriously. It is all a game. It is all like a dream.

******

Who does not want any thing; he is a Dev/evolved soul. In life except God, one should not desire any thing. If he really succeeds in this then he will have every thing. If you don't get success it is your "Prarabhat". Under these conditions the remedy is "prayer" to Almighty.

******

To recognize the self "praise" is the worst enemy of the devotee.

******

Consciousness is always under the control of Ataman/soul. By actions/Karmas, one cannot approach Almighty. One has to cultivate the qualities as that of Almighty to get merge in Him.

******

World and God are the two banks of river. One cannot be on both the banks simultaneously.

******

In this world anger and lust have some limitation but not the greed.

******

God resides between two thoughts; in that vacuumed when there is no thought; i.e. in a "thoughtless state". When all thoughts dissolve; a perfect silence appears; one gets merge in glory of Atman.

******

We miss the presence of God like that of air since it is present everywhere. As without air we cannot live so without God we cannot survive. God is self within us. We arise from God; exist in God and merge in it; like all gold ornaments merge in gold finally; so, we made of God, merge finally in Him.

******

There are six Bhavas of God, namely: prosperity; dispassion; virtue; renown; glory; and wisdom.

******

Brahman precedes time, it is internal. As one gets knowledge of Ataman/self, impurities disappear.

******

In general, one must follows the path chosen by intellect. But when intellect finds it difficult to choose a clear path, one must follow his conscious.

******

Jnana/wisdom arises from pure knowledge, pure awareness and pure consciousness. Consciousness has no knowledge in itself. The consciousness, however, remains as the undiluted witness of all activities.

******

The host of semi-gods and sages represent the cream of creation, the subtlest, noblest and the best. However, the greatest personalities are fall short of Brahman. Once they reach Brahman/ God, they become one with the Brahman/Almighty.

******

22

Life is an Eventful Cycle

Life is just an event in of eventful cycle in the infinite stretch of happenings in time frame. You will perceive to have surrendered when you know your life is insignificant in the span of time and space.

******

Don't feel that you are somewhat different and separate as you are the part of cosmos.

******

When you know that you belong to some one or something mighty then there is no fear as cup of water feels "I am in the ocean"; and water in the cup perceives that "I am the ocean", only then it gains strength.

******

It is wonderful to know that if you happen to love fearful picture, fear disappears. If you love Goddess Kali, fear cannot stand, it vanishes; since it is the same energy in Kali that manifests as fear or love for Kali.

******

Kali means darkness, which is the mother of light. There is darkness in eyes. Through that darkness you see light as pupil of eye is dark and one can see light through this. So, Kali, the darkness, is mother of knowledge and light flows through it. Hence, surrender and love for Kali, pray to make us brave, enlightened and fearless in life.

******

When you are happy in life, feel grateful to God. If you are unhappy, go out and serve someone selflessly; you will become happy. Only when you worry about yourself, unhappiness comes and fills your life.

******

One is encapsulated ocean living outside the ocean since more than 80% of the part of body is water. He is always in God, wherever he is, whatever he is. Same way as fish exists in an ocean.

******

As you separate color from the wall, color would cease to exist. So all creation would cease to survive if separated from love of God.

******

Fish out of water is the shell of fish life and not the fish. One can take/remove fish out of water, but not the fish itself. Similarly one cannot be detached from Almighty God.

******

Duality comes when you divide. You are not separate from the whole existence. You are a part of whole.

******

The food we take, it becomes flesh. In due course, only a matter of time, when it becomes body. So, entire world is like our body. That is cosmic consciousness. Every body is a part of Almighty God.

******

We all breathe in same air. Same air flows in every one of us. So, whole universe is same and affected under the similar conditions. Only the evolution of each one of us is different. Toxins are taken by trees everywhere and we get fresh air to breathe.

******

The more one knows the more unknown remains in him. Gradually unknown grows but he does not grow. Wanders, all of us accept easily, and generally we don't seek answers. If one does not know and talk, words follow him. If enlightened man speaks on any subject he does not know, talk follows through him. It will be some thing fresh and most creative. On the contrary, when one knows and speaks, it will be stale talk.

******

Love, cannot be practiced, it is spontaneous. Similarly, truth cannot be practiced, it can be cognized, recognized, felt, experienced, and lived moment to moment.

******

The feeling of helplessness can lead to frustration or prayers to divinity. When you feel helplessness from the core of heart that is prayer. It can transform life. It can bring force and prayer within.

******

If one knows things, it is not intuition. Maintaining innocence in spite of intelligence is wisdom; it is enlightenment. Innocence is love.

******

Ego separates. Keeping distance is a sign of built in ego. It is unnatural separateness. Egoistic don't consider others as his part.

******

When intelligence and innocence go together, a divine beauty is drawn in behavior and thinking.

******

When you recognize, feel and perceive that everything is impermanent. You will gain strength, and fear in your life disappears.

******

Earlier the human mind was simple, close to source and natural in his approach. Today it has become much more complex, confused, clever, knocking with negativity. One has to hang even to handle normal activity/issue. Moral door was automatic to open but today even by force it is difficult to operate. Even in sleep, world moves in head because one is deeply steeped in every phenomenon of existence. His communication is through many doors. Moral door is generally jammed. Door of inner world is closed. Even when one trusts, he trusts with million doubts in mind. Man does not how he feels and what actually happening in his inner world. Only an unseen power is maintaining the order for everything around us to make the life wheel to move.

******

The world needs innocent people. Everyone feels mental distance from other. No one perceives the part of single divine identity. Every one identifies him self as separate egoist identity. Intelligent people have done more harm to the world. The requirement of innocent and intelligent people is the answer. Confusion all around indicates that prognoses knowledge has broken. One needs to learn again the basis of lost disappeared knowledge.

******

Coming back to the source is the nature of everything in creation. Every thing comes out and goes back is the circle of rotation.

******

Action does not always represent the truth of the state of being. One's own expectation and judgment cause irritation.

******

Human mind, which is stressed and tense only judges; discriminates; loves this; does not love that; makes number of boundaries; ifs and buts; doubts; and then removes itself form existence with no creative decision.

******

When joy become painful or touches its extreme, dispassion begins. Dispassion is that delicate balance, which is beyond both joy and sorrow. In dispassion nothing can shake/disturb you. Dispassion cannot be learned. Your conditions/sufferings/ circumstances can bring. It comes by meditation or by itself. Dispassion is by itself the highest wisdom or the wisdom appears when someone is in dispassion. Man of dispassion is the richest.

******

We are a part of this existence on the whole. Our separateness causes fear. We are the part of earth and ocean. Our every cell is the part of these giants. Our body contains more than 75% water. Same air comes out and goes in the body. No air is being generated. Trees are only recycling the air and make air useable for us. Similarly, our mind is a fragment of the expression of whole big and great mind, and is the creation of this vast universe.

******

Life is a phase between activity and rest. However, we only take life as the combination of activity and rest. We miss the phase, which is the source of "latent" energy for evolution. That has to be trapped to become motionless bodily, and mentally, by entering the era of silence. The pulse between "rest" and 'activity" functions in this gap, is termed as life. Life is neither activity nor just rest. It is the gap between the two. Life can heal itself. In general, spirit of life develops mind, body and retains it. Eventually spirit separates body and makes our system to work through mind and other means.

****

Seed has every thing. Entire structure of plant is present in seed in un-manifested state. How plant develops from seed; what is in side; it is a divine miracle. In the same way DNA contains in every cell of us and it has programmed of our being.

******

The change in consciousness and mind means total/net transformation and not otherwise. This is possible through meditation only.

******

You need to observe fear as to overpower it. Fear can only be overpowered just by observation one pointedly considering this as a part of God and perceiving impermanent of life. Basically, nothing can be held in life, it will just pass.

******

One is born to cry in life. Even after birth one cries. If you as a child have not cried, your parents would have positively cried.

******

In life one cannot cultivate the sense of belonging, if he drops the stresses and fears. Sense of belonging, fears and stresses move together, they live together. All these come automatically.

******

Life is all over. All of us are filled with life and we are floating in life. If this understanding comes, you and I disappear in time.

******

We belong to entire existence. We are not separate from each other. Our breath/air, which goes in and come out from us, can travel though out the world. The same water by evaporation spreads through out. The same is true with mind. Mind is a part of big mind and great mind and is not located in one location. Basically, it is like electromagnetic field. It is present all over.

******

If you are in anguish, you need love and support. Master just takes anguish and garbage, which you cannot lift off. All enlightened masters on this planet are garbage collectors. They do nothing other than being collector of garbage. Masters make us happy after taking our bad deeds on themselves. Master is medium like rains, which take water from sea and pour though out the earth. It is the greatness of Masters.

******

One must not surrender to the criminals. They will only exploit you in long run and you have to suffer sooner or later.

******

If innocent person just tolerate in life sufferings given by others without his faults, then certainly with time his sufferings will completely destroy the others.

******

The main cause of disturbance in life is stress and lack of co-ordination and interaction. The individual peace in society and collective peace start from where we are, and what is our evolution. However, meditation and breath management are very helpful to maintain peace in life throughout.

******

Intake of food in life has major influence. It has in general intoxicating effect, and spoils Sato Guna in the body. So it should be taken in least quantity just for physical needs. Intoxication effect of food gets multiplied in the body and physical condition of body deteriorates.

******

In life, it is easy to adapt virtues but it is very difficult to leave vices existing in mind. These are needed to burn by the power of meditation and required to be washed by God's blessings.

******

When you are clear in mind, you will have good and healthy feelings and vice versa. Crystal clear clarity and devotion are prerequisite for development of healthy feelings for any one, and for any activity. When you are true to yourself in your upright mind, and when mind is unexcited, calm, and serene, then only true commitment, right direction, and correct vision in your life arises automatically for creative useful work.

******

True vision in life gives right direction to your life force. In confusion, vision is always lost and you will even forget it; and then the life force disappears consequently. As a resultant, the inner state of consciousness is lost. Only silence of mind will restore the lost consciousness and bring back the memory lost. In fact the beginning of remembering is the beginning of relieve and restore of vision and life force in the body.

******

When you are unhappy then you are less forgetful. But in joy, you tend to lose yourself. If you don't lose yourself in joy, you will never be unhappy either.

******

23

Relationship

The more advanced we are, the more we face the challenges and problems in relationships. No tribal societies have problems with relationship. Animals have no problem. Nothing is permanent in any relationship. If relationship comes from the level of sharing, then it can last somewhat longer. In general, every person needs relation. In society no one can live without relation with others. Relations are mutable; with time the same relationships are never maintained; even love relations are not forever.

******

To maintain relationship, one needs lot of patience; self sacrifice nature is required; it needs to look after and care for other interests and deep understanding of other person's inner personality.

******

Relationships are like tender plants, they need lot of attention as plants need sunlight, fertilizer and water. Similarly relation needs close attention; inward love; selfless service and not only outward co-cordiality only.

******

In general all relations are very short lived. Relations are governed by mind and its thinking; its inclination is very mutative; and this effects one's behavior as time depended phenomenon; and consequently all these aspects influence relations.

******

Too much closeness in relations is very unhealthy. Sufficient gap in interaction needs to be maintained. For good relation, frequency of thinking and interest must match for prolonged and healthy relations.

******

To have good relationship with all, our best efforts, God's blessings and His Wish play a very important role.

******

The economic independency, lack of common sense ethics, deterioration of value base thinking, and moral ethics disappearance in society are some of the root causes of breakage of early relationships.

******

Living with self and considering others having same divine nature, respectful attitudes for all specially for our near and dears, forgiveness attitudes etc. give the strength in relationship. To forget the past unhealthy experience and live in present adds to improve relations. One must consider that all are not equally evolved and mentally developed and most of them are self centered only; to deal with them and have good relations is a walk on the steep road with great patience and sacrifices.

******

24

Means and Approach to Deep Sadhana

Mantra is nothing but a source and means to be with mind of a Sadhak/spiritual aspirant. On becoming one with the mind, Mantra must be dissolved by itself in Self and become part of it. Mantra must originate from the navel centre; initially mind must listen it deeply inwardly through ears than just whisper before it become one with the mind; and later its vibrations get dissolved in cosmos through apex centre after it turns into divine light in the Chida Akasha on crossing Unmani Chakra.

******

Blind faith need to be developed on Master for spiritual progress, but one must be very careful in choosing Master. Having blind faith is prerequisite but one must be quite sure that on who he is having blind faith is not spiritually blind; he must be enlightened.

******

Biggest and highest blessings on a person are if he is assisted by God to follow the divine path in his life. All other showers on him are just materialistic, transit and mutative only.

******

The physical death of the human body is when it gets disintegrated into multiple pieces. Then it cannot function. But death of the mind is when it is fully integrated and completely concentrated. Because mind lives in fragments; in pieces; does multiple activities; and it is present at multiple places in no time. However, when it is integrated/concentrated, it disappears. It means Maya/ illusion disappears, and supernal appears. Human soul joins supernal either in the Nirvikalpa or Savikalpa Samadhi. Disappearance of mind is the aim of Sadhana and God's realization. Longer the duration of disappearance of mind, more the time one is with Almighty/ God.

******

Religious man is he, who can sit within him and does not need any external company of any kind. He is self -sufficient. He is alone but he never perceives loneliness.

******

Japa/repetition, the name of Almighty/God is most significant and important since it is the bridegroom in one's marriage. Without full integration of Japa of God in the mind, mergence is not feasible. One may have every thing but not the bridegroom then marriage cannot be performed.

******

When man dies, his subtle body or Suksham Sharira from every part of his physical body leaves or gets disintegrated from the physical body. It is very painful like a surgical operation. That is the reason that man becomes unconscious before death.

******

Writing autobiography has no significance, if one hides the negative side of his life. Every one certainly has both positive and negative sides in his life.

******

God is Karta/doer of every thing as reaction of one's actions/ Karmas/deeds. However, He/God can easily rectify, if He wishes even after execution. That is His greatness. He is the supreme authority.

******

A man must lead inward and outward life for all round spiritual progress. Those who lead only outward worldly life become money monikers. They will have lot of wealth along with all worldly comforts but not peace in life. On the contrary those who lead only inward life become monk with time; however they will have peace. One must choose middle path and lead both internal and external life in a balanced way to be with God internally and earn money by right means in the external world. Basically wealth of external world and inner peace of God inwardly is both divine. Both must be worshipped and treated with due respect.

******

Those, who are always busy throughout the day with external activities, don't allow their mind to relax and look into the depth of their mind. Their mind behaves like a monkey when they are alone without external work. Their mind can never be in peace with inward probing. They cannot take inward spiritual journey and suffer with various mental and health ailments in due course. One must always spare time to sit with the self and observe his breaths every day to be in peace and to make all round progress in divine and worldly life. To be silent without much external communication preserves internal energy to be channelized in various positive directions.

******

The void appeared in cosmos is by cosmic energy, cosmic power and AUM vibration of very less amplitude having high frequency. In the time frame of billion of years, AUM and AMIN vibrations generate sound energy without any rubbing that might convert cosmic energy/power gradually into the fire, which might turn/ transform into gas in long run and expand/spread all around. When it travels a long path in cosmic void, it losses its energy gradually and get condensed, which take the form of earth, planets, stars and various other asteroids. These might break with time and this process goes on and on. By cohesion, by colliding and collision of various asteroids, planets etc, electromagnetic spark may get generated, which might give appearance of different species in the universe. Still the question remains unanswered that from where this void, energy and vibrations and so on get generated, which result in formation of electrons, gases atmosphere and so on. The net phenomenon is beyond apprehension of little human mind.

******

In the human system, presence of life force/pranic force with the aid of immense strong AUM vibrations might get disintegrated that might generate cosmic power, cosmic energy and cosmic divine light in the human brain. This is possible by Yogic Sadhana of various kinds and by practice of deep meditation leading to absolute mental silence. Only then this divine cosmic light is emitted from the human skull or apex center that lead to ecstasy/ Samadhi/mergence with the supernal and mind may be extinguished temporary. Only under these conditions and by the grace of Almighty/God this divine cosmic light with soul energy travel upwards and merges with the supernal cosmic energy. This is complete transient breathless state and this only happens in the state of suspended breath. It may be the state of awareness in the beginning and might turn to be the state of partial awareness in due course. Gradually, remaining pranic energy, that is not converted in divine light returns back to the human system and body function starts by itself with awareness as earlier. The state of complete unawares is the state of Nirvikalpa Samadhi. One enters to this state fully only after physical death.

******

Man lives in repetition. He breathes repeatedly. Eats the same food again and again. Every thing is repetition. One cannot live without repetition of his activities again and again. "Mantras" and God's name are also repetition. Chanting of these churns the system and leads to generate energy like in "Samundar Mandhan" i.e. churning of ocean water. This energy finally may enlighten a person by Almighty's grace. In Guru Granth Sahib, the holy book of Sikhs, there is mostly repetition of God's praise in different ways, words and forms. Day and night, months and years, all are in cycle of repetition. Thus the life of a man, which is endless cycle of repetition till he is liberated from the cycles of birth and death.

******

Intellect/mind and heart/emotion are the basis/core of material and spiritual world, respectively. Mind is above animal instinct but much different than emotions and pure heart. Science and mind are superior in external world but these are not comparable with religion and God. Mind needs to be dissolved to be with the God and to make dent even to conceive spiritual sciences.

******

Along with mind, eyes are the basic prerequisite for understanding science and experimentation etc. But to understand religion and spirituality, the capacity and power of deep listening i.e. healthy ears are most essential requisites that lead to deep understanding and thinking. Deep listening is extremely difficult. Listening should be so deep such that listening must create vibrations in the navel centre and should be able to generate Udana Prana, a source of spiritual energy in the system that awaken the kundalini power, which after climbing to apex centre may merge with the supernal and aspirant may get self –realization by the blessings of Almighty/ God.

******

When one wants to speak, vibrations are generated in the navel centre. When these generated vibrations reach through heart to throat, Besant is created and by this Para Shakti/power/energy; emotional words appear in throat under the influence of pure heart; and then we speak through mouth very loving and pleasant words, which touch the heart and mind of the listener. On the contrary, deep listening is in reverse order that create Udana Prana in the navel centre and it may create emotions if words touch the heart provided words are from the heart of the speaker. Otherwise it will be just mechanical listening only.

******

There are five types of tar pans/debts for an individual in his life: namely for Petra (ancestors who are no more); food for hungry person; care for plants & animals; created life force by spiritual efforts and its mergence with soul; and our deep silence to Almighty/ God.

******

Even good and bad actions are just created by thinking. Bad thinking by mind creates sins. One has to suffer mentally as reaction to his sins. Wrong deeds give physical punishment, but wrong and bad thinking give us mental harassment and problems in due course.

******

For mergence with cosmic power/energy, mind is to get separated from life force and breath has to get seized by it self for the blissful state to appear. Under this state Nada/divine voice transforms to Ana had/silence, and the realization is experienced. Only under this achievement, life force after transformation from Udana Prana passes through coccyx, sacral, dorsal, lumbar, and cervical and medulla before it merges with supernal and divine blessing is poured through apex centre to the devotee.

******

Sun/ light do not know what darkness is. Darkness immediately disappears as soon as light/ knowledge/sun/ Guyana appear.

******

In this world man changes only the shape of material to make different products; it means material shape changes. Basically there is no alteration in the existing elements of the material. Gold being same can be transformed to different ornaments; ocean remains the same; the change occurs in the wave pattern. We have to live in this turmoil only. We are the part of this great worldly ocean. Ocean will never be perfectly calm. Life diminishes in time frame and reappears again and again with different varied evolutions.

******

For our survival, we don't have control on air, we breathe. We don't have control on water, we consume. We have only little control on food, which we take. So food must be taken selectively and judicially to be healthy and gay. On one side food is diet to live, it also acts as medicines to keep us free of diseases and control them accordingly on the other hand.

******

In human life there will always be miseries and troubles of one type or the other; no one can escape these, living on the earth surface. So, we must take vertical journey to be above all types of troubles to have peace and balance in life and thinking. In other words we must be detached doing all mundane activities of life.

******

Yug changes as per the thinking of the majority of people. Yug change is the cause of mental inclination of majority of population. There is no change that occurs to plants and animal kingdom with this change. Sat yug is the Maryada Yug. Shri Ram has followed ethics so he is known by the name Maryada Purshotam. Lord Krishna period was Leela Yug. Truth has been sacrificed in this period. Weapons were used to save the devotees. Present period is Kal Yuga. Majority of people are matured to handle any activity even by unethical means. Present society is a mixture of different class of people. Some follows ethics of Sat Yuga, Some follows medium path as in Dwapar Yug, a few belong to Treta Yug and still some have light of ethics but majority has no values in this period of Kal Yug. It is period of full of desires and Tamo Guna.

******

25

Deep Mystery of Parapsychology

The astral body turns into spiritual body at another ethereal plane in the penultimate stage. Then the spiritual body turns into soul-form, which can penetrate into infinite cosmos beyond any physical inception. Finally soul form gets into timelessness

****

Outer vision is a mere physical perception where as inner vision is psychic phenomenon. Furthermore, inner vision is intuition and thoughtless–centre less, and traverse is soul-supernal linkage.

******

Beyond the re-clam of psyche, there is no existence of sin. And beyond spirit there is no virtue. Spirit-Supernal is above all.

******

Every breath is a craving in material horizontal world. It creates hope and finally throws us in the ditch of memory as misery even after success or failure. Life must be detached for craving of this or that to follow the vertical journey.

******

If one achieves the art as to how to suspend the breath, then time becomes a void for him. He enters into timeless state. In fact void and breath are anti-poles.

******

To condemn is easy but it is most difficult to condone.

******

In absolute term life is around desire, decay, degeneration and death.

******

Love basically has no form so it cannot be ravaged. Love is beyond desire, word and meaning. Love is mystic, it binds not just two but it is capable of binding the entire cosmos as one.

******

Introspection is silence in loneliness but meditation is silence in aloneness. It is a pathless path and stateless state. Meditation is the creative dynamism that surpasses all limitation of time-space and consciousness. It is beyond acting, reacting and enacting; it is beyond forgetting and remembering; it is floating in myriad –heights of the sky of the skies; it is to enter in the abode of silence where only life force is active and rest of the system gets commanded.

******

Every cell of the body is a culmination and vine-section of bio-spiritual, bio psychic and bio-somatic forces.

******

One must make meditation as the effortless flight by practice and Almighty's grace. Gradually awareness shall be dropped in meditation as the mind is annihilated. Then only one becomes fragrance without being a flower. He is transformed as a branchless-tree of light pervading in the birth-less sky.

******

Every thing turns to be the same when one travels at a higher plane and even concept of suffering disappears. One has to transcend the mind beyond pain, pleasure, peace and bliss. Mind is like lame leg; it cannot climb the tree of light/realization.

******

God is your ship that sails you safe to the shores of unmitigated bliss. There is no other short cut to reach Him except to sail in His ship, which is by His own Wish and Blessings.

******

One must never say good-bye to the failure in life. Any failure teaches us humility. It is the nature's gift for shedding ego. It should neither be cursed or nor should be willfully invited.

******

Having uplifted the inner life-force with the grace of Almighty/ God/Cosmos, the three–coiled serpent awakes up and gains momentum on climbing up, and when it reaches the tri-junction situated on fore-head in between eye-brows, the third eye opens up unfolding the chapters of seeing, seen and seer. Then only the spiritual aspirant merges in existence as the flying and floating bird of light. Basically, rhythm of life force takes a flight into era of ethereal silence.

******

Visions, ecstasies and intuitions are mere accidental outcome and non-essential bye products of meditation. However, the sole purpose of meditation is to merge as a nameless losing every entity in the infinite Cosmos; the stateless state.

******

In general, knowing is half reality, being is full reality and integral is whole; from where there is no return/come back.

******

Godhead is a stateless-state. If one attains this state, he is bloom forth as a flower of silence. Then he has nothing to express, nothing to manifest and finally nothing to lay claim over any thing.

******

Expectation is not the certainty in life; prospect is only prelude of truth; real travel is that which has no prior knowledge or hope.

******

If one has to beg, he must beg the mercy of Almighty God. Whose grace is infinite; benevolence is oceanic; and compassion is sky like.

******

Life is not mere taking breath and leaving. The mystery of life is too complex and much deeper than one can even perceive.

******

God is our anchor, bay and shore. We must make Him our navigator and leave every thing to happen according to Him; His design; and His scheme. We must never try to make them happen with our power of ego; it may turn our life into an epic of unforeseen tragedy.

******

Maya/illusion is an unresolved mystery. Human birth is a manifestation of Maya. It is also a part of Brahma. It is Brahmin manifestation. Maya is very strong and very powerful as God; God creates it; it can only liberate us and can merge us in divinity of God. There is absolutely no way of realizing God without the mercy of Maya. One must worship Maya as Cosmic reality. We are prey of Maya; it is always there to control and grab us. To get rid of the clutches of Maya, one needs lot of efforts; God mercy; and co-operation of Maya/illusion itself. One cannot come out from Maya just by knowledge. Only meditation is helpful to make Maya somewhat ineffective.

******

Time itself is a mystery. It is illusion/Maya. Time is a tool to cross over to the domain of timelessness. Timelessness is the very essence of immortality. Feeling of timelessness is meditation. Time is a replica of eternity through death.

******

Spirituality is not the path to the bed of flowers. It is full of thorns. Only faith can transcend all these.

******

Absolute silence is beyond the reclaim of awareness where there is no time, no breath and there is no motion. It is complete void.

******

Life is a pilgrimage of evolution. It is rhythmic momentum of the wheels of the chariot of life force. This is all through the grace of that un-manifested unseen source-light.

******

The conversion of energy to matter is evolution but of mysterious order; however transformation of matter to energy and beyond is of much higher ascent. This needs lot of efforts, patience and preclearance.

******

When AUM is heard, it is cosmic cause and it is "SAVADA OM". When AUM is beyond hearing, it merges into silence, it is cause of cause, and it is called "AVADA" AUM. Transformation from SAVADA to AVADA i.e. from listening to silence is the traverse towards meditation.

******

Through meditation, life force structure is broken in to the tiniest form that can easily merge into an integral whole of cosmic–luminosity. Until the total mergence is not completed, ascent of life force in meditation is not total. There are seventy two thousand nerves that take the life force to every bio-atom.

******

It is experienced that any fluctuation of the uniformity results in the misbalance of the psychosomatic–spiritual equilibrium.

******

Higher stage of meditation consists of generating the unique solo rhythm of life force, which gets channelized through the ascending trios i.e. Ida, Pingala and Sushumna. Straight posture is maintained throughout that lead to transform after years of practice to turn life force into divine light, where efforts and consciousness get merged and spiritual aspirant enters in stateless divine state.

******

Meditation is basically freedom from the known. It is timeless traverse in the trackless timeless path. It is beyond seeing, perception, hearing, knowing, action and beyond any conceivable cognizance. Finally it is beyond peace, bliss and perfection. It is stateless state, and pathless path. It is culmination of merging beyond the awareness of attainment and fulfillment, and is of beyond description. Nothingness is very essence of its form and formlessness. The secret of meditation is to float in this state for a while to be with the unmanifested existence.

******

The sitting in meditation is a potential dynamism of the creative silence. Meditation is the evolution of every bio-atom of the being into the divine light. It is the source of joy, the joy being in existence but beyond expression. It is the source of absolute silence.

******

It is for us to serve the nuances of Maya—the illusion. Out of this cosmos it got manifested and we are part of this. The only way to merge in Brahman is through Maya.

******

Whom you serve is not matter but how you serve shows your inner built- up.

******

One must serve mother earth, nature, saints, and miserables. Serve those that belong to God, serve dielectrically opposites also considering them as a part of God. Always consider "To Serve is an Opportunity".

******

As there are four openings of Sri Chakra, so there are four modes of worship. The first one is outer ritual i.e. Bahiryoga—the worship of outer Cosmos. The second one is the worship of inner Cosmos. The third one is the secret worship by name Rah yoga, where inner and outer get merged. The fourth one is the most sacred worship of effortless naturalness.

******

You must perceive that you possess everything yet you should know that you own nothing. This is the real dielectric of Cosmos. It is evident that you own the breath so you survive. Until you know how to disown the breath, the source of breath will never be revealed to you. You own the soul, unless you disown the soul for a higher purpose, it does not get revealed. Similarly when you disown your name, form, perception and your penance for the purpose of mergence in the source light, you are likely to possess every thing.

******

One must be very clear that life is a pendulum between living and leaving; one's birth is not an event but his mergence shall be; living alone is beyond sin and virtue; getting beyond awareness is real floating.

******

The reason to be certain is more valid than being certain, yet certainty is built as a co-ordinate beyond reason. That is whole secret of dielectrics of mysticism.

******

Reason beyond reason is always grilled, persecuted, butchered in the hands of savage i.e. majority of cowards, hypocrites, looters and rulers.

******

One must experience that there is ever moving invisible power behind every type of evolution; it is the nameless spirit. And one must harness that spirit for cultivation of inner and outer peace.

******

The invisible void may begin to explode bit-by-bit and atom-by-atom any time. That is the real threat, which is set to operate. How and why is a mystery beyond mystery?

******

Faith is propagated beyond reason and religion; it emanates out of moments of void/nothingness. It is the choice-less act of silence and that is the source of creativity. In silence breath is suspended leading to the stillness of void. Transit dimension between breaths to breathe is being in void and in the era of time-less-ness. This state-less state of an individual is the state of cosmic one-ness.

******

God is creator, creation and created. He sends us in this world and wants us back to Him but the ways, means and clues to get back are hidden/concealed in His fist. God is not a concept. He is mysterious beyond. God is neither the form, nor the formless. He is beyond both.

******

All unique and creative things happen in silence. To achieve silence is subjective. It cannot be taught.

******

Some define God as formless void. He is a stateless state of bliss. Only when one sheds memory and awareness, vertical path to ascent towards God becomes feasible.

******

Breath is virtually a secret of wisdom. When it traverses downward, all primary instincts get aroused. When it is in lower middle, secondary emotions follow. If it revolves around upper middle, psychic emotions appear and when it stands in Visuddha centre, one gets the glimpses of Absolute and when at tri-junction—journey of ascend begins.

******

26

Avadoot Geeta

Interval between two subsequent breaths is Sandhya. This gap/ interval is meditation. This Sandhya is vacuum. The Sandhya beyond Sandhya is light; which is neither word nor meaning; it is beyond; and that beyond is called mystic beyond; and that mystic beyond is a void; and can be reached by mergence; and nothing else.

******

Even the awareness of breath after some time is dropped. The object of senses is attracted by senses only provided there is strong breath. If the strong breath is made feeble breath by awareness, the senses for go the capacity to attract action or reaction.

******

If there is no thought then there is no mind. No mind means that mind is concentrated/one pointed, and that is the beginning of meditation. Thoughtless state appears when breath is suspended or when breath is feeble. No memory, no past, no future, only "now" is the origin of meditation. From here, ascent of divine light commences. Becoming/experiencing void on the mental level assists for mergence with the supreme reality in the end. And this is the highest achievement of life.

******

Renunciation of thoughts, which existed, cultivated or built in knowledge and ego might assist for mergence in the Absolute.

******

There are 24 Tat /factors exist:

1. Organs of perception (five) are hearing, touch, sight, taste, and smell;
2. Organs of action (five) are hand, feet, tongue, reproduction organs, and evacuation organs;
3. Tan mantras (five) are smell, touch, sight, taste, and sound/ hearing;
4. Gross elements (five) are air, water, fire, earth and space;
5. Subtle elements (four) are mind, buddhi, ego and prakaruti/ nature.

******

When mind evolves or merges for enlightenment even for a moment; it gets transparent quality of reflecting Brahman at that moment; but soon after it withdraws into the prison cell of horizontal activities/limitation; it starts behaving like a mad dog as it was.

******

For spiritual progress mind is to be annihilated and it is not to be relied upon. Every one of us is the prisoner of his mind, but it is considered as if he is liberated. Once the mind's awareness is dropped, mind is vacated and only then it is completely annihilated. In sound sleep, mind is fully vacated and we enjoy perfect and complete rest. It is the case of transcendental state. Mind can talk and perceive shape, size and so on. But it cannot point out light since there is no meaning of shape and size for light. It is always boundary less.

******

Once the void within is created then the light of Ataman is filled. This leads to the appearance of silence within, which is beyond bliss; and after this the soul realizes its infinite nature. Then qualities of soul get manifested gradually and all inlets of the void are closed and there is no re-entrance of mind in this void of silence. However, if there are gaps in the void and void is not continuous, and then mind creeps in like a thief. It resides in that void without allowing the void to co-exist there. Void is total thoughtlessness state i.e. no talking, no thinking and even no seeing within. If the presence of mind is felt; it must be allowed to ascent vertically; and then it will disappear by itself. Under any condition it should not be allowed to revolve as thought. Mind cannot hold one idea for more than a few minutes. Without shifting its focus mind cannot exist.

******

All that is created must be excluded and annihilated by discarding the mind. That is manolaya. Laya leads to Maha laya. Maha laya is Samadhi. Mind must be turned vertically upwards into void, which is the zone of silence. Even breath is needed to vacate to be in void, which is created momentarily only. In the traverse of void, i.e. the silence, if the stabilizing of light takes place, then it is the enlightenment. However, if one merges in void, it becomes non-void since it becomes full. Hence, the thought of even mergence is to be avoided. One must touch the light only but higher awareness in the arena of silence should be avoided. One must know that without mind, he is pure soul. Without awareness, one is nameless experience and without experience, he is light. And if light is taken away, then he is Brahman itself. If the awareness is withdrawn, the world becomes illusion, and what remains is God/Void.

******

As long as consciousness is there, world exists, and so the memories and miseries. Mind is a basic cause and soul is causeless. And once the soul as source light in the finite being is released, it attains the stateless state. There will be either mind or enlightenment/light. Both cannot exist together. When objects do not attract mind, mind vanishes, and finally light appears. It is like coconut water inside the coconut, layers are to be removed to get water/light.

******

Udana prana/vayu gives inner spiritual energy, and it has to be generated in the navel centre by mantra Japa. This gives fuel to Kundalini for its skyward journey. This makes a spiritual aspirant thoughtless and arena of silence appears. Act of meditation helps to reach in that state and afterwards as one entrenches in that state of silence, he rises himself above the action. Finally one crosses the awareness of the subtle state to be in Savikalpa Samadhi.

******

As the life force is released from apex centre, feeling of weightlessness is felt that is the symptom of being airborne. It happens in microsecond. It happens by the light, through the light and in the light. It is void/shuniya state. It is the state of mergence, which is contradictory to immergence/ Maya state. Under this state entire body becomes function less, and only light functions

******

HAREEM is the same as RAM in Hinduism, as RAHEEM in Mohamedanism and AMEEN in Christianity.

******

When Life force is duly regularized, it churns a type of fire in you, which produces necessary heat that consumes both organic and in-organic impurities within the body. And when life force/ light goes out through apex centre, then one is in Avadhuta stateless state. Here light acts as a charioteer and mind as chariot.

******

Mind is a combination of time, space and consciousness. In deep meditation, when state of time less-ness appears, space loses its concept and consciousness disappears. This puts mind in closed door and temporary it is locked and loses its significance. And era of light spreads all around in Chida akasa. It is basically an UNMANI STATE. It is a state of no-motivation, no desire, no duality, no trinity and no misery.

******

In the state of feeble breath, awareness by and large is disappeared. However, this feeble breath is sufficient to ignite the light in us. We can ascent the light/life force and this will act as breathe also. Nothing happens even if heartbeat slows down to the maximum extend. In fact by vacating/suspending the breath, void appears, awareness disappears and light merges

******

Five elements i.e. earth, water, air, fire and sky are closely linked with awakening, dream, sound, and trance or chide Agni and mergence, respectively. Light/Life force becomes pure when it transcends all the five elements and merges with cosmic energy.

******

Mind can be easily controlled through number of breaths and breath pattern. Breath of 21600 per day can be reduced to 1000 to increase longevity. To preserve breath directly means to preserve energy. One must vacate the breath as many times as possible to achieve Shunyaka. Then mind becomes silent. Silence is bliss, it is Brahman and it is mergence with the Supernal. It is above time, space and consciousness. Our knowledge is below this and so we cannot understand Almighty. We can only merge in Him.

******

With practice of meditation, one loses awareness gradually. In practice, meditater, object of meditation, and process of meditation are merged, and silence/void in mind prevails; and mind becomes intuitive. Void means silence and is not just emptiness. If silence is felt as known, then it is illusion, and if it is unknown then it is God/Brahman. God is neither conceivable nor inconceivable. It is the merging point of the unknown.

******

When during evolution of spiritual aspirant, life force is emerged; it undergoes all types of worldly awareness as it traverses. Awareness is a breeding place of memory and memory is the mother of sentimental attachments.

******

Meditation should be emergence. But generally it is withdrawal, annihilation; vacation of thought; breath; sight; and all sensing receptacles.

******

Emotion is nothing but awareness with time, space and consciousness.

******

In relative terms of wakeful state; dreamy state; deep slumbering state; and Turiya state; Brahman is in a stateless state. It is thoughtless thought; nameless name; and a formless form. It is basically light of all lights. It is a state of silence of the absolute.

******

The crux of the problem is awareness even during the time of meditation. No body tries to drop the awareness. They want to enhance the awareness. Meditation starts with full awareness but in deep meditation, awareness must be dropped. Without awareness, as pure light, sky-ness journey is accelerated at Unmani where silence becomes/turns into light. Any experience in the vertical path is awareness, be it joy or misery. With this dualistic system/pattern, it is not possible to realize God. Awareness has to be dropped for self-realization. When mediator/ spiritual aspirant is totally inactive in physical activities; he is without awareness; then only inner light may become active and mergence may be enhanced.

******

Imperceptible nature of light makes sky to look blue. It is space and part of illusion/Maya. By wisdom light cannot be created. It appears in unaware silence by creating void in the stateless state of suspended breath.

******

Avadhuta is a form of Brahman since his spirit, thoughts, and breath revolve around only the Absolute, and not around relative cosmos.

******

The mind is born by breath and if one succeeds to vacate the breath, all other fences will be demolished naturally. Vacating the breath creates void and light appears. All techniques including increasing gap between successive breaths and length of breath etc. revolve around the creation of void and appearance of light.

******

Brahman is Creator, Sustainer, Destroyer/withdrawal (Maheswara); and Sada Shiva with Sivani is for Emitting/re-creating the world; it is Kameswara.

******

Atomic structure; principle of antimatter; existence of sub atom; and foreign alien unknown forces are yet not understood. Atom sprung from tremendous unknown energy source, which is still a mystery. It merges back in the same nameless energy source.

******

The realization and enlightenment bring very vividly to us that we are not the doers; things are done through us by the grace of Almighty force. Guyana/knowledge is a stick in hand while moving in dark but if one has light of realization then no Guyana is needed.

******

No performance either outer or inner shall lead us ultimately to Almighty. They can only push us to inaction through this action. Manifestation of Brahman is Maya/illusion, and that is mutative aspect of Almighty. So material and all actions are Maya due to Brahman.

******

Soul is nothing but the collective luminosity of every bio-atom in us. In meditation, scattered energy from the cells is withdrawn as light and sends to the various centers of the spinal cord. Only by deep meditation through prostration of silence, Brahman is reachable; merely with positive viewpoint and approach, He might not respond.

******

Mind has no capability to probe into unknown. It does not know the way. When mind is mingled and merged with Udana Prana, it turns into life force then only it can probe by entering into the silent zone of Chida Akasha.Only Udana Prana turns into light and can have skyward journey.

******

Human mind being non-self; it cannot reveal self; if the mind is pure then there is no difference between mind and supreme being; both become same; mind is merged; self and mind become illuminated; then no further practice is required to purify. When self is filled by self; then there is no meditation; but if our experience in universe is not the self, then we are not in state of meditation and Samadhi.

******

It is indeed wonderful to conceive that the self, which is consciousness itself, can never lose consciousness of its true nature and therefore Samadhi is superfluous since Samadhi is total mergence and there is no consciousness and not self remains in Samadhi. In Samadhi light is merged in supreme light; no consciousness; no awareness; no self; and nothing in Samadhi; so it is superfluous before death till some one is alive; it is virtually a paradox.

******

Sambhavi Initiation is the highest among all types of initiations; it is just by touch; by look; when highest knowledge is transmitted to spiritual aspirant by self-realized soul.

******

It is amazing and mysterious to know that spoken and unspoken are not the complete/absolute truth; and nor the known and unknown are. If there is only one indivisible; all comprehensive absolute; then how can there be objects, senses, mind and intellect. It means there is existence of Maya/illusion; the supreme manifested force; like indivisible un-manifested absolute.

******

For Avadhuta; there is no rebirth. Each letter of the word AVADHUTA can be depicted as: A: free from bondages; pure; VA: with no desires of any kind, DHU: free from all diseases; no meditation needed; TA: truthful; free from ignorance; egoism etc.

******

27

Unknown Mystery of Life

Awareness and mind have only finite capability, they cannot be aware of infinite—the Almighty.

******

Sooner or later one will understand that breath is an existence and gap between the consecutive breaths is enlightenment to the self. Basically existence is a meaningless periphery over the mystery of the unknown. Furthermore, death and living have no relevance; these are mere existence.

******

Remembering God is basically serving God. To search a path in the desert of life is not a problem but to get destination, an oasis, is the real issue in life. There is never part achievement in the temple of God: it is either full or nil.

******

The void always turns into crisis. Crisis is the crucifixion of self. Every one of us is a Christ unless we die to that past and pain: there is no resurrection; resurrection is the Christ – Consciousness. Life always offers a choice but crisis overrules it.

******

True faith acts as a flower in life but fear is always a thorn; it always pricks. However, in true flower of love, separation acts as a real sustaining factor to move peacefully.

******

Pain in life must be taken as a passing experience. But constant awareness of pain is a defeat in life. No pain in life is a total loss and no gain is a total gain. All is relative.

******

Faith can definitely be created if one looks within for the unknown forces; he will be amazed.

******

Every thought that persecutes, takes away the chunk of energy, which comes from the unknown. However, strength is inherited from the known; it is relative; but energy is a divine gift from unknown.

******

Life is not a proposition of loss and gain in vertical traverse but it is fundamentally true in horizontal traverse and well being. However, ultimately material and mental gain has no place: one must die for his belongings; for his dependence; and for his mind. To be self-realized, one must learn to die before he finally dies/ leaves his body.

******

One must not be eager for recognition of his talents by others. One must not keep balance sheet for loss and profit; as well as for pain and pleasure for spiritual vertical journey in life.

******

Life force, mind and perception must turn into unified field of dynamic silence to get mergence of your light circle into the apex light.

******

Unless one is prepared to accommodate and show due respect to higher values of life, the very hope of survival of humanity shall get buried.

******

One will experience in life sooner or later that fate is paradox of circumstances but fortune is an uninvited guest. It comes of its own by mysterious path unknowingly. Fame is basically outcome virtue of fortune. This may be termed as destiny and is not made by desires. It is by the wish of Almighty.

******

Without patience, nothing can be achieved in life; without efforts nothing can get fulfilled; without God's grace nothing happens. That is why God's judgment is mysterious beyond the concept of human mind.

******

Since every thing is created by Almighty; it is part of Him; the only way that He could give to a created being such as feeling of individuality; separateness; it is through Maya—a cosmic illusion.

******

Cosmic delusive force is Satan; it is created by God. Satan is working through disease, mental sorrows and satiety. If God destroys Satan, it means He is going against His own power.

******

Earth, water, air, fire etc. are different states of divine vibrations.

******

One will never see faults in others in life if same seeds of faults do not exist in him. This is the law of nature.

******

Matter is a frozen energy rather frozen consciousness of God. However, life force is semi consciousness.

******

An ideal wife should be wise like an elephant, pure like dove, loyal like dog, affectionate and home loving like pigeon and sweet like nightingale.

******

It is physiological and psychological fact that consciousness and energy must be drawn up through the spine into the medulla oblongata in order to merge into the infinite cosmic energy for self-realization. During its travel to infinity, it passes through coccygeal, sacral, lumbar, dorsal, cervical centers before going to medulla.

******

Only higher spiritual experiences can withdraw the mental energy from the temptations of sex. In other words when Kundalini current passes through brain, desire of sex disappears.

******

Due to the manifestation of vibrations in body elements comprising of earth, water, fire, air and ether, liking for different tastes and colors of sweet/yellow, sour/white, red/sour, blue/sour and bitter/extremely sour are gradually developed, respectively.

******

As waves are the part of ocean so the matter is the part frozen spirit; only its amplitude and frequency of vibration vary. Every thing is a transformation from one form to another. What one loses in finite life, he gets in the chamber of infinity. Life is in changing form as water, ice and steam. Change and expansion of consciousness is required to perceive one-ness in many-ness.

******

As often as we think wrongly, the whisper in the temple of silence and wisdom guides us to the right path, which leads to thee. One, who seeks prosperity for themselves only, becomes poor with time. Seeking prosperity for the complete world, will take him to thee.

******

In general, intelligent people are born poor; and mentally unhealthy born rich in prosperous families.

******

It is well known that our physical body is just the materialized energy. If so, then how could energy be sick? It should not be sick. If it is sick then it is clear indication of improper distribution of energy and should be rectified by various means of allocating energy properly. Also, after many years of deep understanding and various means and practices, one can learn how to be healthy by contacting and trapping cosmic energy. The means and tactics are to spiritualize the atoms of the body so as to get rid from the diseases. Once the life force is separated from the body, integrated it with the cosmic energy and re-absorbed in the body, finally this will make the body healthy with vitality and grace. Human consciousness that is located in the body and Christ consciousness, which is between the eyes brows in the center of fore head can be with appropriate means be used to canalize the life force.

******

When one enjoys vast internal joy within himself then he is in cosmic consciousness and do not depend on external means for his joy and happiness. When one does every thing for the joy of others without any selfish motives then he also enjoys the cosmic consciousness, and touches the heartily feelings of others. The extended state of this consciousness without affords are the superconsciouness state and this can take him easily afterwards to the Christ consciousness, which is the light of intuition.

******

There is a deep rooted karmic reason for chronic ill health and repeated failures in life. One must tense and relax; exhale several times as and when fear comes at any occasion in life. Under no condition, one must infringe upon the right of others. It must be known that if opportunity comes then it must have been created some times in the past by the self alone. One can himself realize that if one contacts God first then every thing will follow without problems.

******

Meditation is the missing link between religion and realization. One cannot effectively meditate without quieting the breath flow, heart and lungs. Contracting muscles of the chest and then tensing them again help to release energy, which can be canalized for meditation.

******

The life force can assimilate oxygen more quickly in the body than liquids and solids. Also, a person while fasting can charge his body with electrons and free energy from the air, and even more by certain breathing exercises.

******

When one is relaxed then oxygen and blood are not required in that part of the body, which is under relaxation. Under these conditions that part of the body survives by getting life force from cosmos coming down from medulla oblongata.

******

In Savikalpa Samadhi, one is only aware of God where as in Nirvikalpa Samadhi, one is aware of both God and universe. It is the state when eyes are half opened and half closed.

******

Liberated person lives in the world but he is not of the world. Liberated man joyously, consciously, fearlessly and painlessly leaves the body without any attachment. He annihilates the mind when he is alive. With all this, he is never insincere.

******

It is unbelievable for most of us that a man dies when life force retires from the spine, brain and particularly from medulla oblongata and then decay of body continues. Basically cessation of heart beats and breaths are not initial symbol of death. These follow afterwards. Auditory faculty (listening) goes last of all dying men. Life force is retained in any of the seven centers before it leaves. It leaves from the muscles first, but as the life force leaves the body, there is a transition of soul from physical body to the astral body. Death is a physical metaphysical experience. Only the enlightened one rejoices the freedom of soul leaving the body through medulla.

******

It is better in life to be unhappy of your ignorance than to die happily with it. One must not go extreme of any thing in life neither spirituality nor for material gains; adopt the middle path. Mind, matter etc. all are vibrations of different and complex pattern. To Wish and to Will, have also frequencies with different phase and amplitudes. Higher Will is the Will of God and that is most powerful.

******

One must contact God in the temple of silence then only health, prosperity and wisdom will be added. Meditation is the only way to go back to God. For any good work, one must feel that God is working through you. Magnetic power of God in plants contacts carbon die oxide, water and sun rays to grow and give fruits.

******

If one thinks constantly for God or chat His name, spiritual magnetism is created like passage of electricity creating magnetism. By this one becomes divine magnet. This magnetism generates love for God in him and vice versa. Love creates/ exchanges magnetism for God. It is this magnetism and flow of current in thoughts, which acts on chemicals in body that charges the battery of human life. Various thoughts are produced as vibrations of power of this magnetic energy. In fact words are vibrations of these thoughts. In a pure mind and heart, thoughts and words are closely linked/co-coordinated.

******

Mere repetition without understanding deep meaning of mantras or incantations does not produce results. It is effective when one is totally merged in the vibrations of Mantras and listen them deeply with depth of mind. This increases the spiritual sensitivity and then only individual consciousness projects into the space and into the hearts of other human beings.

******

On reforming the self, one can reform thousands around him. As one progresses in divine communication, he will easily go on well with every body. As one comes closer to existence; the changelessness; then all divine qualities are added to him. One must get answers of all queries from himself; then only he will be accomplished and prosperous.

******

All our actions are governed by certain laws. Nothing happens in our destinies just by chance, or because of circumstances outside us. To some extend we can trace our own cause effect experiences by introspection and impersonal analysis. We all are children of God, but unfortunately we have chosen to play the role of beggars in our life.

******

The dreams signify the state of one's consciousness. One must adjust his waking thoughts and actions if he wants to improve his dreams. Most of times life energy is withdrawn when one dreams, so he does not remember dreams.

******

Evil tendencies from prenatal existence and bad company have the worst influences on human conduct. Under these conditions God respond through laws and not through blind prayers.

******

A worn out body can rejuvenates by changing its atomic vibrations. Condensed atomic energy is given to the body by the pure food. Fingers act as antennae and one can feel the energy flowing into them.

******

Relaxation, when precedes meditation, is the way to infinite. God being candle flame cannot withstand the gust of restlessness. When the storm of breath is stopped, ripples of all type of sensations will vanish. And this experience, which is not forgotten; is ours; the experience that is forgotten cannot be ours; it is just the memory.

******

Life is a wave of electrons and atoms; a wave of protoplasm; a wave of power; and a consciousness. Life is comprised of electrons, life force, intelligence and soul.

******

In death, the power of touch goes first, and then vision, then taste, then smell, and last of all, hearing.

******

Your success and failure is the result of past actions. What are you today is the net resultant of the past. The unity of purpose can never come if selfishness is piling up in the heart.

******

The five existing currents in the physical body i.e. Prana is for crystallization; Vyana is for circulation; Samana is for assimilation; Udana is for metabolism; and Apana is for elimination. All these currents are generated in the body by the mysterious activities of breath in the system.

******

Spirit is without motion. It is vast infinite stillness behind every thing. When some one is totally still like rock then only one can visualize the passage of cosmic energy entering the body through medulla oblongata, and it can be directed mentally where ever required/desired.

******

Mostly people have evil habits because they do not know the greater charm of good divine habits. Ignorance is a mother of all anger and evils. One will not commit errors if he really understands the miseries and troubles, which his errors and ignorance will bring.

******

To be in meditation, the breath will be suspended temporary and concentration prevails. In deep concentration soul is not in contact with senses; it is in his divine nature. Heart beat reduces to the order of 50/minute.For a peaceful person like Napoleon and Duke of Wellington and many advanced yogis, heart beats are bare minimum: less breath and more divine energy. Only when venous blood flows back towards heart, then heart palpitates and allows the life current back to medulla, and breath continues.

******

The more body lives on life force, the less food is needed for survival. In human body four forces are active i.e. breathe, life force, mind and vital sex energy. Each cell of these fluids/ energies acts as a condensed electrical battery.

******

Breath is a cord that binds the soul to the body. When man learns to rise above breath, he ascends into the celestial realms of angels. This is the only way to keep the body rejuvenated by uniting human and cosmic consciousness through meditation.

******

True success in life depends on the balanced life of meditation, intellectual studies, health, happiness and earning a livelihood in truthful manner.

******

Almighty takes away material things, comforts etc. occasionally from any one; so that one is not earth bound, but he should be detached. And real spiritual truths cannot be effectively taught by one who has memorized, but by whom who has experienced and understood.

******

As waves cannot exist without ocean and so a man (wave) cannot exist without God (ocean).

******

Cosmic sound can be caught only when the heart radio of deeply meditating devotee is tuned to the frequency of divine vibration. He, who knows God as the cosmic sound, finds himself free from all the limitations of miseries and death in the world.

******

The purpose of religion is to expand the human consciousness until it unites and becomes one with the universal Christ consciousness as Jesus and Krishna did. Thus, as one loses attachment with the world, he becomes a Yogi. He develops intuition gradually as a result of pure reason and calm feeling. In fact intuition is the knowledge from within and does not depend on any data offered by the senses or mind. It is a state of super perception; it gives feeling of deep joy; beyond the reach of senses. Faith is closely related to the intuitive perception. It makes one happier day after day. Intelligence, extended by meditation, becomes boundless intuition. Thus if one experiences the cosmic consciousness even for a minute, he starts loving every body; every creature of the universe; as His manifestation.

******

Solid, Liquid and Gases can be linked as life, thought and feeling aspect of human existence. Illumination, light, enlightenment is the energy, and/or frozen vibration of God.

******

It is wonderful to know and perceive that "A Breathless Silence" is the only passport to enter the astral world. Also, finger tips are very sensitive to direct where the souls of departed lovers are.

******

Success in life depends upon the ratio between past success tendencies and present judicial efforts of Will for success. Success consists of — in the ability to destroy all the apparent tendencies of failure by the power of super concentration. The energy felt in between the eye brows must be switched to the brain and hold there for long time. In this way the vital power will roast all lurking disease seed tendencies from the past, and thus tendencies of ill health and failure can be controlled.

******

Spirit has no alternative consciousness of wakefulness and sub consciousness like that of human being, but has perpetual, enjoyable, active and inactive wakefulness combined within itself. The spirit is basically knower; the act of knowing; and the thing known. The spirit only differentiated Him self in this way for a cosmic entrainment. Spirit has created many images of the self like jeewas. Cosmic delusion, or Satan, is the conscious imagination of spirit willing to make Himself look finite, where as in reality He is infinite. If finite is tuned with infinite then there is no problem/fear of any kind. All worldly problems including war are cosmic delusion. Satan through the power of sex keeps the kingdom of inharmonious finitude.

******

All diseases are because of broken laws of physical, mental and spiritual in harmony.

******

Thoughts are more important than actions because these are the forces that instigate actions. Before actions are performed, one has freedom. But after action, effect of action will follow. One must be calmly active and actively calm. Calmness is one of the attributes of the immorality within.

******

Super conscious mind remains buried beneath subconscious mind, and sub conscious mind buried below conscious mind. However, sub conscious mind takes care of the working of organs like heart, lungs etc. even during sleep. It is always awake. On the sub conscious mind screen dreams are produced whether they originate from conscious, super conscious or sub conscious mind. Super conscious mind can work with conscious mind and sub conscious mind without getting entangled with any one. Super conscious mind expresses the pure intuitive consciousness of immortal soul. The super conscious mind uses the brain energy and shows the image what is going to happen. Furthermore, at the advanced stage, when a true vision is seen with open eyes, this shows that life force has been projected from the brain into the ether. Seeds of evils in sub conscious mind can be roasted in meditation while in contact with super conscious mind. Sub conscious mind acts as refrigerator and like a store house in real life. In general, all troubles of life are because of under developments and lack of intuition.

******

Cloudless sky represents a serene pure path of communication with God. Appearance of light, sky and ocean represents vast perception of self realization in meditation. Also, when one dreams and witnesses calmly ocean and vast sky etc, this indicates that effects of bad karmas are getting worked out.

******

Protoplasm is the medium through which life force creates living bodies by cellular division and multiplication.

******

Unless a man frees himself from compulsion of sex force, he cannot liberate his soul. Spiritual transmutation within Will can control sex impulses. Continue inhale and exhale, and some times by force exhale of breath helps to transmute the sexual impulses and negative/evil thoughts through change of frequency pattern of the fine internal forces of the system. Sex temptation cannot be controlled by sending the life force/current back into the heart and by uniting this with brain current. Evil thoughts are most powerful of man's interior enemies.

******

One must know his own personality: spiritual; business like; selfish etc. It is best to know the individual personality since it is formed through sprouting of seeds of action left from a previous birth. Man's own action in previous birth rather than heredity determines individual traits. All prenatal habits can be changed by cultivating wisdom by meditation only. And physiological changes occur in the body by Will power when no impurity inside and outside of body exists. To develop a specific personality if one wants to develop, he must absorb the desirable characteristics of that personality by constant attentive association. Furthermore, one acquires the qualities, he admires in others.

******

One must be humble instead of egoistic, and through the magnetism of humbleness one attracts friends. As on a peak of mountain no rain water can stay, so on an up rust ego no water of knowledge can collect. Furthermore, egoism is born of an inferiority complex, which may appear as superiority complex, where as humbleness is born of wisdom and knowledge of one's truo oolf.

******

One himself is responsible for the environment around him self; this has been created by him consciously some where some times in the past; so, present conditions are the result.

******

In meditation, if one sees golden ring, this represents and gives indication of cosmic energy; and the blue sphere in the golden ring represents the Christ consciousness. By piercing the blue tunnel, one can enter into the white star tunnels gradually in the Christ eyes and then in the cosmic eyes; and by rays in cosmic eyes the devotee penetrates the wall of matter; thus he reaches to the Absolute—the UN manifested kingdom of pure ever-new blessedness of spirit. In this circle of blue is a reflection of the soul light. In soul light, existing spiritual eye can act as broadcasting station as well as intuitional source. Furthermore, who is able to penetrate the star in the spiritual eye, can project his consciousness into the spiritual eyes of another person.

******

All auditory, olfactory, gustatory, tactual vibrations can be changed by concentration into visible, optical vision in the spiritual eyes. In deep meditation, when eyes balls turn upwards, then soul through life force pass unconsciously out of medulla oblongata to cosmos. The spiritual eye is actually the reflected light of the medulla. Light is basically seen in medulla oblongata, but devotee think it is in between the eyes brows. One must expand this light beneath, front, behind limit-less Ely until one is with infinity; with cosmos.

******

In Cross, the horizontal line represents the finite world; or nature; and vertical line represents the infinite. When these lines are crossed, they symbolize the cross between nature and spirit. We are the product of both finite and infinite. The realized super man withdraws all rays from the nervous system and floats them through spine and let them out through medulla oblongata into infinite sphere of light.

******

The goal of life of all beings consists of in acquiring peace, satisfaction, safety, consciousness, knowledge and immortality. It is a voice of God and by this He calls us back to His mansion of oneness. In early age only prenatal tendencies and their influence is predominant but as one grows social and family characteristics begin to exercise.

******

A human being is like an upturned tree; the hairs and cranial nerves are roots; spinal cord is trunk; and different nerves reunifying from them are the branches. God has created man for reasoning and woman for feeling. As per Bible, the serpent is the out going current of life energy stimulating sex energy. The garden is human body; trees are various nervous systems; fruit is sensation. To dic mcans to love/merge with consciousness. God desires that man may enjoy all fruits of senses except the fruit of nerve tree of creative force i.e. sex. He can enjoy within norm sight, smell, hearing, taste except the touch, which is the radiance power.

******

By deep meditation, the body loosens its atomic vibrations and becomes life force. The astral body changes to ideational body and further Christ consciousness via ideational consciousness. When consciousness of astral body vibrates and changes the vibration of all atoms, then one hears only cosmic sound and become one with the holy vibration. Christ consciousness is the reflection of cosmic consciousness. By meditating on spiritually advanced people, one gets their magnetism. Spiritual masters look from within to without where as others looks truth from without to within.

******

It must be clearly perceived that food charges the body battery; concentration charges the mental battery; where as spiritual battery is charged by divine wisdom. Rubbing head and body generates life force; this can be easily experienced by spiritual aspirants.

******

One must not accept the integrity of associate very easily. Eyes are the index of mind. If one finds shrinking of eyes of an associate on seeing through them, then one must be careful about his intentions. Some times just closing your eyes will give the innermost feeling of the associate. Generally spiritual people, being honest, are easily deceived.

******

28

Sacred Divine Waves of Upanishads

Self is caught up in perception, emotion and thought. Body, mind and intellect cannot perceive, feel or comprehend the transcendental. Even terrestrial experiences are difficult to describe as they become subtler.

******

There are five activities of pranas namely perception, excretion, digestion, circulation and thought absorption.

******

One cannot feel God with mind and nor conceive Him by intellect. Brahman transcends the known and the unknown. He is beyond all that is known and all that is unknown.

******

There exist four sources of knowledge: Pratyaksha-direct; Auman-inference; Upama-comparison; Agami-tradition and intuition.

******

The main purpose of idol worship is to grow out of it, to leave it in due course.

******

Conscious is subject and not the object. Organs of perception can perceive the sense objects but not the consciousness, which illumine them. For this attention must be shifted from the object of perception to the subject perceiving.

******

Prana is the electrical gadget and the consciousness is electricity. Electricity is the primary cause of functioning of these gadgets. None of them can function without electricity. The consciousness sustains by itself.

******

The self is not something that is felt or known or experienced. It is being. You become the self just as dreamer becomes the maker.

******

One has to leave mind and intellect before entering the premises of Abode of God as one has to remove the shoes before entering to the temple. Since self lies beyond the realms of known and unknown.

******

Through senses one perceives, through mind one gets thoughts and emotions, and through intellect one gets deep thoughts. All these three constitutes the world and worldly affairs.

******

Self realized man has disinterested interest and dispassionate passion towards the world's affairs. On the contrary, the less evolved is more attached to the world. If one is more peaceful then only he is more objective and efficient to his work/action.

******

He, who loses his life for His/God's sake, shall find it. He, who finds his own life for himself, shall lose it.

******

After acquiring the knowledge of the scriptures and exhausting the bulk of vasanas, desires, the seeker has to practice concentration and meditation. And wait for silence for the ultimate experience. In the moment of absolute silence, the seeker gains enlightenment. The gap between efforts and enlightenment is the wait age passion of the seeker. In fact spiritual pursuit does not commence until one is freed from viciousness.

******

True worship is subjective by mind and intellect, but other types of worship by sense organs of action and perception are objective. Idol worship is Saguna Up asana, where as Nirguna Up asana is formless worship, which is the highest. Pure light is not visible. Only scattered light is visible. Similarly unknown Brahman is known through the expressions of the knowledge in the world.

******

For virtuous, the voice is low and clear. It takes one to the right path. For the vicious, the cloud of desires renders the voice faint and feeble. One must know that the world emerges from Brahman, exist in it and merges into it. Brahman is the substratum and substance of the world. The body, mind and intellect are ever changing so the perception, emotion and thought. For recognizing the changes, there must be a changeless substance. As moving trains needs immovable rails, so changeless, immovable Brahman is belonged and recognized by changing world. Brahman is like sunlight. It is every where but does not move. Only conditional Brahman i.e. Maya/illusion, moves but not the unconditional.

******

By renouncing this material world, one can enjoy peace and bliss of the underlying reality. Renunciation is possible when one escalates to a higher position. One cannot detach if he is not attached to some thing higher.

******

Mind is like a fire. It will consume any amount of fuel and is always ready for more. Only when mental desires are minimal, reaction is feeble. Furthermore, self less actions performed in a spirit of service and sacrifice do not stain the personality with vasanas and desires. Cycles of action/reaction will not end unless desires are exhausted.

******

It is obvious that no pole-volute can cross the bar without the help of pole. Ironically, no pole volute can cross the bar with the pole. So, all paths need to leave the support of practices for achieving the final goal. Any practice belongs to the world only. It will purify the mind. Practice has to be left as one succeeds to uplift him. Only purified mind can meditate.

******

The practitioner following the spiritual path, if falls, he plunges himself into thick blinding darkness even much greater than that into which a materialistic man plunges, if falls.

******

Basically there are four different ways of getting knowledge:

Direct perception by senses; Inference i.e. by indirect ways (like fire and smoke); Comparison using various similes and metaphors; Traditional i.e. knowledge by saints and sages.

******

Jeewan Mukta means spiritual enlightenment in one's life; where as Videhamukta believes that enlightenment comes only after one cast away the physical body. The total extinction of the individuality is known as "Mahasamadhi".

******

Prarabdha is a part of Sanchita i.e. reserve of virtues and vasanas. And consciousness functions as a self in all beings.

******

God has five attributes:

Omnipresence: Val our; Fame; Affluence; Knowledge; and Detachment.

And qualities of devotees are: Vivek/discrimination; Vairagaya/ dispassion.

Sadsampatti: Calmness; Self Control; Self-withdrawal; Endurance; Faith; Tranquility. &

Mumukastava: Desire for self –realization.

******

Heaven and hell are not geographical places but mere mental states. The state of ecstasy is like heaven and state of agitation being hell. One attains ultimate enlightenment under totally desire-less state with no agitation in mind at all.

******

UN manifested hidden fire manifests in a piece of wood. The fire, when generated/manifested, consumes the wood. This UN manifested fire in the wood represents the self. The hidden fuel in the wood is like the matter layers comprising vasanas, desires. The invoked self i.e. fire destroys the vasanas in the individual. As both fire and fuel are contained in the wood, similarly Jiva houses both spirit and matter.

******

Awake is gross state (bodily state), dream is subtle state, deep sleep is causal state and thoughtless state is blissful state. Beyond waking, dream and deep sleep state is Turiya, where in lies immaculate self, which is substratum—the individual consciousness. There is no agitation beyond deep sleep; it is blissful state, all agitations cease there.

******

The infinite springs from finite. As one seed creates tree, number of fruits and seeds and so on. Infinite actions, thoughts emanates from self Ataman. As one becomes self realized, he turns himself to the state of pure consciousness, and then he sees self and self alone. He can only access the knowledge of self. Self is the purest. Purity indicates the absence of otherness.

******

Existence/non-existence is intellectual concepts. Brahman is beyond conception. It transcends the intellect. Hence, it is said to be beyond existence and non-existence.

******

The mind and intellect perish at the moment of self realization. But self remains the same. It is immutable and imperishable.

******

Earth is inert but vegetation is alive. Camphor (Kapoor) used in pooja/worship represents the fire of knowledge destroying the vasanas.

******

It is said that if coconut breaks in two halves, is auspicious. Uneven breakage indicates gloomy and disastrous situation.

******

OM is the bow, the self is indeed arrow, and Brahman is target. One with steady mind should become like an arrow. The more bow is pulled and arrow is sharp, it can penetrate easily and can merge with Brahman. This all means that there should be perfection in spiritual practices/efforts to penetrate and to achieve desired goals.

******

As dreamer can awake so the seeker can become Brahman but cannot perceive, cannot feel and cannot comprehend Brahman.

******

Meditation is the art of focusing mind on supreme and finally, at the peak of meditation, the seeker drops the final effort and plunges into silence. It is like a river merging with the ocean; then it is like cessation of even efforts. It becomes similar to a pole, which is used to climb at a height and finally to drop it to jump to the other side. And that is the side of enlightenment.

******

29

Wonderful Heart Touching Quotes

Death is not the greatest loss of life. The greatest loss of life is what dies inside us while we live. And the secret of success is the consistency to pursue.

******

It is worth and wonderful to know that attachment associated with want is desire; associated with success/getting it is elation; associated with uncertainty is anxiety; associated with not getting it is depression; associated with inference is anger; associated with somebody else getting it is envy.

******

Every thing comes if a man only waits provided he deserves. Only the 10% of life one makes it, 90% he takes it as comes.

******

Beautiful things can not be expressed. These can only be felt. Only the man of worth can recognize worth in another man.

******

Ability alone is not enough for success. It must be sparked by ambition and sustained by determination. Ability becomes useless unless it is properly used. It is fine to have ability, but the ability to discover ability in others is the true test. Generally, a superior man is distressed by his want/lack of ability. Lastly, ability is of little account without opportunity.

******

If some one accepts you as you are, he will make you worse; however, if he treats as through you are what you are capable of becoming, he helps you to become that.

******

We judge ourselves by what we are capable of doing while other judges us by what we have already done.

******

Generally, one thinks according to his nature, speaks according to conditions and acts according to built in customs.

******

Broadly, life is a misery to be born, pain to live and trouble to die. In life one does not decide his future, he decides his habits and then the habits decide his future. So, even death is not to be feared by one who has lived wisely. Furthermore, neither the embodied mind-intellect nor Atman ceases at the time of death.

******

He who can, do; but he, who cannot, only teach.

******

To get angry is easy, but to get angry with right person, for the right reason and at right time is really difficult.

******

The only conquests, which are permanent and leave no regrets, are conquest over self.

******

A timid person is frightened before a danger, a coward during the time, and a courageous person afterwards.

******

A lie has speed but truth has endurance. There is nothing permanent except the change.

******

It is important, not to curse the darkness but light a candle. Every noble work seems to be at first impossible.

******

To be persuasive, we must be believable. To be believable, we must be credible. To be credible, we must be truthful.

******

Nothing is impossible to the person who does not have to do it himself.

******

The greatest achievements have always been individualistic.

******

One must think like a man of action but act like a man of thought.

******

The purpose of life is life of purpose. One must know what he wants in life, emotionally, materially, physically and spiritually. If he does not know where he is going then how will he ever know when he gets there.

******

Air, fire, water, earth remain in space, and space is the subtlest. Self is far subtlest than space, and cannot be destroyed by any means. It is internal. Also, Brahman exists without the world but world cannot exist without Brahman.

******

The cycle of nature remains undisturbed i.e. sun/heat converts water into vapor, vapor is transformed into clouds and then rains, again water, heat and so on....Similarly from flower, fruit appears and from its seed, again the tree grows.... So manifest nature of Almighty is changing, is mutable, it is ASAT, where as UN manifest is changeless and SAT.

******

Through constant and consistent meditation, the individual drops his causal and subtle bodies and become united with the self.

******

Where there is time, there is death. Beyond time, there is no death. Annihilation of mind is peace. Peace exists when mind is transcended.

******

Kesava is another name of Lord Krishna, which means a dignity with luxuriant hairs.

******

If mind is not purified, it will slip from Mantra recitation. It cannot be concentrated. Concentration is never at one particular spot in the head. It only turns the gaze slightly upwards, which naturally generates a feeling of devotion.

******

Attachments are generally because of past. Desires are because of future. Realized soul is free like child since there are no attachments and nor desires.

******

This world is not real, nor unreal, it is mithya, the Maya; an illusion that creates delusion.

******

We being of infinite stature; so we cannot be happy until we merge in infinite. Unless all the three Gunas i.e. Sato, Rajo and Tamo merge, we cannot be realizing Brahman. It means we have to transcend all these Gunas.

******

If a man starts 100% discriminative action with 0% impulsive actions, he gradually becomes emotional. Eccentric and insane is 0% discriminative and 100% impulsive.

******

The ignorant is often the most adamant about his opinion. Also, superstition can victimize some one when his intellect does not function. When emotion overwhelms a person, he is in no condition to listen. He becomes depressed when emotions over power him.

******

A person working for higher ideal is never tired. As Lord Krishna—the Krikesa; the lord of senses. And Arjuna –the Gudakesha; conqueror of sleep.

******

The process of birth and death goes on until your last desire is exhausted and your mind, intellect merge with soul; and you become one with the supreme self. Desires are due to imperfection, incompleteness, or unfulfilment within. It is the root cause of emotions. Only wrong relationship produces misery. If one drops clinging attachment to the world, one lives life of peace and bliss.

******

Maya, the illusion is neither real nor unreal. It is away from both. The same one experiences in the transit world.

******

Desires are perceived by senses, mind and intellect. They are mutable and changeable. Only self is immutable. All phenomenon repeat from UN manifest to manifest and back to UN manifest. This cycle repeats endlessly in nature. Then why to grieve?

******

Sankhya or Sankhya philosophy is the linkage and sequence of logical thoughts arriving at rational conclusions.

******

Action performed with selfish and egocentric desires creates fatigue that never gives happiness in life. A higher activity is always beyond personal liking/disliking. Unattached and impersonal work is real satisfying work in life.

******

When one leaves desires, he becomes detached, dispassionate, in different towards the experiences of mundane world. This indifference is an essential prerequisite for plunging into meditation. However, mind will have two types of movement, one from place to place and secondly within a place—it moves at the point. When mind become silent, intellect becomes silent and this accumulated silence then reveals pure self.

******

It is wonderful to observe that when a flower grows into a fruit, the pedals of flowers fall away. The process cannot be reversed. If pedals are plucked to accelerate the growth into a fruit, the fruit will never immerge out of a flower. The pedal-flower-fruit growth is similar to that of spirituality.

******

The important facet of self control is: when intellectual discrimination rather than emotional feeling decide one's activities.

******

Happiness is a relation of number of desired fulfilled to the number of desires entertained.

******

Without intellect, one is under the guidance of feelings and emotions; when intellect completely vanishes, he meets with disastrous.

******

One must mentally annihilate desires to remove their roots. If he physically annihilates desires by external self control and not mentally, he will jump in desires as the situation comes. Actions done without attachment, destroys the desires and one can reach ultimate state of perfection.

******

Curve of the river can never turns right angle but gently takes right turn. Similarly one cannot force people to follow him, but gradually and slowly can convince them to follow.

******

Sattvika is like smoke on the fire, which can be removed by wind till one becomes self realized. Rajasika is like dust on mirror, needs cleaning. Tamasika is like embryo in the womb, it takes lot of time for transformation.

******

Spiritual knowledge can be imparted only to the extent one has unfolded the self.

******

One is never in state of objectless, thoughtless, emotionless, awareness less every time; he is in conditioned consciousness.

******

Brahman with name and form is matter; it is Maya/illusion. So UN-manifested Brahman is Almighty, and manifested one is Maya. So God and Maya/illusion are one and the same.

******

Structure makes a difference whether diamond or coal; both are Carbon.

******

Self through ever inactive but it is nevertheless the primeval source of all actions as electricity, petrol etc. It is immaculate. The self within is paripurna/complete; whole; perfect; absolute; and infinite. The self; God; does not interfere at all with our choice of action.

******

The inherent tendency of man is vasana. Vasana is the cause; and action is effect. Again action becomes cause and vasana as effect. It goes on. Vasana produces thought, and it results in desire and that finally leads to action. However, birds fly in sky without leaving any traces of path i.e. without any vasana. Virtually this must be the way of human actions and vasanas.

******

He who sees action in inaction, and inaction in action is a wise. Wise one merges with self and becomes witness, the sakshi. Self expresses through causal, gross and subtle bodies. One never knows that he is pure unconditioned consciousness. One revolves around conditioned consciousness.

******

Wise follows the path/action to renunciation and from renunciation to self-realization. Renunciation is the effect after following the path of action. Resultant is achieved by efforts, devotion and God's grace. One has to live like lotus leaves, which are born, live and die in water. Yet in its entire life it never gets wet.

******

Ignorant attributes good and bad to Brahman. Brahman has no attributes. All attributes, all qualities, belong only to the world. Karma, Bhagati/devotion and Gyana reduce desires.

******

Indulgence does not bring joy and nor abstinence bring sorrow. State of neutralization is the best middle path to be followed.

******

This world is a play of opposite. It is dual in character. Good and bad move one after the other. Great soul sees their own soul in every body. Upward gazing develops devotion as yoga is service for higher goal in life. Spirituality can only be followed by giving up desires for material and sensual world.

******

Mind will suffer as long as intellect does not confirm to determine course of action. Furthermore mind chants Mantra but intellect only observes it. Mind feels emotions and intellect create thoughts. Mind can be restless, turbulent, or it can be strong and stubborn.

******

30

Sri Sutram & Sri Chakra

The centre-less centre of the nameless void is cosmic energy. Its expansion as circumference is para-sakti. Throb-less and centre-less centre is Iswara. Shri Chakra (the circle of light) is the symbol of the origin of cosmos. Shri Chakra is the replica of the primordial sound in its veracity or cosmic-luminosity. It has nine orbits of cycles. Entire cosmos is a play of light. Void is the matrix of cosmos. As existence is descended out of void, and so the non-existence. Self awareness as the lord of the void is the birth of supreme ego; this is perceived as Almighty. From this awareness of the vast nameless void appear a desire; and if this desire is for association with lord; it becomes Sakti/power or Kameshwari.

******

The perception pull of Shiva and Sakti in union is called Kama or supreme desire. The interaction of anti-poles is the first couple as cause–supreme and function supreme. Due to interaction of anti-poles, some thing like third projection came into being as creation.

******

Sri Chakra is essentially worship of mother–goddess, called variously Lalita; Tripura-Sundari; Shadasi; Rajirajesvari; or merely Devi.

******

Yantra is a device, which helps the regulation of the devotee's energy dynamics so that it is guarded from disintegration, decay and death.

******

The explosion of void is in the cycle; it is as bindu/point; it has spanda (throb) and pratispanda (ego).

******

Ganapathi is a centre-less centre is as Sadasiva and from this static dynamism form, energy spreads like cosmic life force; and thus becomes many-ness from one-ness after traveling through spine.

******

The self consciousness of the void is tremendous life energy. By splitting it into many rays, it becomes Brahma as spread of its glory. That is Shri Vidya as paravidya; the mother of Brahmvidya. Because of its compassion for creation, it is light (with these desires); it is red. Thus it is called Rajarajeshwari, Mahatripura Sundri and Dasamahadevi.

******

Bindu/point/dot is a centre of infinite absolute as mutative energy. The dot expands and becomes triangle by spin, rotation, and by mutation of this permutation and combination; it becomes a womb of cosmos. Triangle is like a womb of cosmic symbol of yoni. Bindu passes through Spanda and pratispanda and expands. HRIM is the symbol of cosmic yoni. Space of triangle inside is SRIM. Thus HA—is sky, RA— are Chidagni and IM—is infinite, so HRIM is Brahma energy. Here AIM is the dynamic symbol of first Yoni i.e. Shiva and Shakti (A and I); M is fire.

******

In each element, half is occupied by the same element; remaining half is divided equally among rest of four elements. That makes one element. For example in earth, half is earth element and remaining half is equally divided in water, air, fire and sky elements.

******

Maya (illusion) is mutative (changing) mystic energy. Sri Chakra is a symbol of mergence and emergence i.e. symbol of Cosmos and beyond. It is a functional dielectric of Cosmos. Furthermore, Shiva is contained and Shakti is container. Lalita is the beyond of beginning-less infinite. Apara is physical Cosmos and Para is beyond of beyond. Matrix of Para and Apara is Paratpara, which is mergence (Laya); and it is Sadashiva. Srividya comprises of mystic secrets of Sri Chakra, Srimata, and Cosmos as concept.

******

The spin of un-manifested Nada (silence) revolves around itself with a desire to create. It is a Shakti. Nada is not sound but a cause.

******

OM-HARIM-SRIM Bijas are indicative of the worship-able creative cause. Where OM is male force, HARIM is female force and SARIM is dissolution.

******

Turiya state is opening of third eye. It is transcendental stateless state. It is beyond knower, knowing and known. SAVODA is chanted OM, where as AVADA is un-chanted OM.

******

Shiva having accepted the desire for creation becomes Jiva. Jiva is like inner God within us as consciousness. And Mother/ Mata is infinite spread of unknowable force.

******

Dream state establishes the relation between macrocosm and microcosm. When center of consciousness as soul suspends its activity towards cosmic many-ness then it is called dream state.

******

Five elements can be coordinated as:

Earth as fullness; water as eternal force; wind as life force; fire as all knowing force; sky is omnipresent force.

******

Life moves in four major stages i.e. creation, existence, extinction and disappearance. And Pran vayu is oneness of life force; mind and soul are, that controls the human existence.

******

Beyond time, space and consciousness, there is void, which is beyond estimate or concept. The sphere above Sahasara is Para; the light spread there as Prakasha.

******

There is no difference between Maya, Jiva and Brahma. But Jiva in Maya assumes an apparent separate entity concept. Maya by ignition of Almighty, transform into matter, atom etc. It transforms into energy. Maya is a dynamic disposition of Absolute; the entire cosmos is the theater, which is the play of source- energy.

******

31

Crisis of Self

Crisis is a mother of failure and suffering. The world is an interval of nothingness in between void and God.

******

In reality any question is a doubt and answer is a reaction in general. One must be beyond both as the silence is only for evolution. By thoughtless silence, one can break every thing.

******

There is nothing like total understanding for any aspect. Even one's own understanding for him self is partial. Nothing can be absolute in real sense.

******

Life is a balancing act. To achieve this one must master his mind and have full awareness. One is what his thoughts are. Causes of agony have been initiated some times knowingly and some times unknowingly. Furthermore, relations are not made on hire and fire basis. Generally crisis occurs when there is the end of faith in one self.

******

One must always remember that any success in life has many fathers. All will claim responsibility for the success but when there is failure in any activity, one becomes orphan. No body will part the failure. One must not forget that this is the dictum of life.

******

None shall live with you in your private hell of pain. You have to live there alone. Any thing is a temporary phase in life. One must try to change it to one's advantage. There lies the destiny.

******

In crisis, anger leads mind-less impulse. One must not react but enact.

******

Pride is a path of nescience. It decides and takes the path as traverse, whose destination is ruin. Pride enjoys its sadist pleasure of hurting others. There is no harm in accepting the temporary defeat and having open mind.

******

Hypocrisy is self centeredness. Its only aim is to gain something even out of sky and winds. Their praise or condemnation is directly proportional to their need based plan-precepts.

******

The root cause of jealousy is not being able to establish inner peace through contentment. To overcome these short comings in life one must observe, learn, feel, think and keep faith in silence only.

******

Pain is the path of life even if it is linked with God. Obstacles and troubles are part of progress. One must not loose sight of one's ultimate goal.

******

One cannot pretend forever of what he really is not.

******

Prejudice may be because of genes. Genes cannot be changed. They can be cloned. Prejudice, without reasons is crime. It is intolerance. It is the root cause of all evils.

******

Fear about fear is only fear that defeats you and persecutes you more than any fear.

******

Frustration is the consequence of accumulated and unfulfilled desires. It is the brain child of fear of fall. It listen to itself and not to any body else. Taking opinion from frustrated man is like taking blessings from widow for a bride who says “Be thou live like myself”.

******

Except hopelessness, nothing for cynicism appears right. If one is not committed to life, the purpose of living is to wait for death.

******

Treachery is expected from people who know strong and weak aspects of your personality.

******

In nature there is nothing constant-constant. It is only variable-constant or a relative-constant because cosmos rotates on principles of evolution. Evolution is never permanent; it is a type of mutation and transmutation.

******

Life always has dualistic possibility. There may be success or failure. Success comes by proper centering and it is because of tranquil breath i.e. equal flow through both nostrils. Ultimately every thing turns into non-existent illusion before final mergence into the absolute.

******

Those, who don’t enjoy silence, are always in crisis. Company of good books and good people enhance silence and crisis gets dissolved.

******

Attachment becomes curse if others are adamantly stupid, possessive and greedy.

******

Real love is not mere proximity. It is mergence of souls in each other.

******

One must not be like donkey and camel helping others in distress. One must help others but try to be in his own silence without much interaction unless it is highly warranted by compassion and faith of the needy.

******

No body knows behavior of one's own in next breath, however healthy he may be. It must be known that there is wide gap between known, knowable and unknown.

******

Crisis is experienced when emotions and intellect get abused or cheated or persecuted or badly suppressed by stronger sadists, cheats and highly selfish people. Crisis is felt when reason fails.

******

No body will agree that most of us are eccentric and are patients of varying degrees on one way or the other.

******

For general average mind people and emotionally oriented intellectuals, the release of tension by satisfying the primary basic instincts including sex is the most easy and adapted way. But higher mind consider sex as a futile exercise. He uses this creative energy for much higher goals in life.

******

Draggers don't think before they talk. They talk and talk before they deplete their energies. They criticize every body and conveniently speak lies. They are impulsive and disown every thing to the maximum extent.

******

Every sorrow and hurt shall bring us closer to God. And every trial makes us grow if our faith in God and soul is true. To practice silence is the A, B, C of spirituality. We must realize that breath is God. We must treat the breath as our closest honorable and reliable friend. This will disclose us the secret of truth and make us happy showing the path of self –realization to us.

******

Most of people around us are just paper flowers. Their appearance is deceptive. Sense-less talking is their past time. They are inefficiently efficient and efficiently inefficient. They are not committal and say 'yes' for every thing but never perform.

******

The aroma of life is silence of non-awareness. If one enhances this aroma, he will come to know the secret of life.

******

Interaction of anti-poles is conflict. Victory tends to forget the conflict that proceeded but defeat has to remember the preceding conflict.

******

The conflicts are of four kinds i.e. between man and nature; man and man; man and mind; and finally man and source (God).

******

Mind plays trick by its own way. No senses/nobody can be above mind, unless its awareness is expelled and annihilated. That is possible only by taming the mind to take up the vertical journey into the unknown.

******

Every thing is ego including breath, birth, desires, positive and negative qualities, expressions etc. Even the faith in God is challenged when mind is in whirlpool of a crisis. Only way is to vacate the breath, to maintain vacuumed to over come the crisis.

******

It is wonderful to perceive that mind cannot live without desire. So, mind and desire is first couple. They are in love and in quarrel with each other. The name of this quarrel is conflict. The fulfillment is only misery.

******

Feelings are root cause of misery and happiness. Neither is permanent. They are mutative. Out of breath, peace, misery and happiness, if breath tends to zero then happiness and misery also tend to disappear. Only peace will exist. Also, when happiness tends to zero, breath disappears. But without breath or with suspended breath, one cannot survive longer. However, vacating the breath in stages is the secret of transcendence living. Thought-less-ness is the cure for all ills of mind.

******

One must be clear that future in any body's life is like a sky. Future cannot be predicted like location in the sky; where one will finally land. Past is sea; where past is buried, it is futile to locate. Present is earth; and every success and failure depends on X- the unknown factor. To make a plan is easy but to implement it depends on various unknown factors.

******

Mostly people surrender to their own ego instead of higher faith, which is silence behind unnecessary reactions to all happenings.

******

Unless the cellular meta- morph-sis takes place at the level of breath; and blood & bodily functions as physical consciousness; no further changes come in other subtle planes.

******

Awareness is awakened by consciousness brought by breath. And awareness is type of suspension in nothingness.

******

Selfishness always thrives like a parasite on others. All relations are based on selfishness. Ultimately all relations are futile.

******

Destiny follows vertical journey and it is ascending form of unknown hope. Where as fate pursuits horizontal travel and influenced by clouds and rains; fate is descending and unraveling. Sometimes fate is surrounded by mystery, which is off shoot of problems those could not be solved.

******

Misery is the best medicine for spiritual evolution and an out look for material detachment. Misery corrodes into the vital energies if it is allowed to spread; at times misery has no solution.

******

By and large subjective stress and greed turn the love into a conflict.

******

In human relations, if scratching gives soothing effect to the itch of desires to each other, it continues to thrive. But if scratch turns into a wound to the other, then existing love gives hatred to each other.

******

The whole cosmos has been sailing in the nameless ocean of void of space.

******

Compassion cannot be crucified. It is the God's grace and blessings of Almighty. It condones the criminals; and it is prey for their enlightenment; it is manifestation of patience and unbearable silence; it demands sacrifice.

******

The mind is both the weapon of revenge and reverence/respect. Selfishness of mind and discontentment move together.

******

Void to void can be conceived as the journey of soul. State of silence of mind is the awakening of soul; and from form to form is the voyage of mind. Space is a void between atom to atom; electron to electron; cell to cell. Energy is drawn from void only.

******

32

Breath–The Invisiable Divine Force/Energy

Breath is God. It is bundle of closely knitted five elements: earth, water, air, light/fire and sky. Breath is also Gayatri—the protector of body as light and light is energy. Our reaction to the situation is directly proportional to the breath pattern. In depression state of an individual, the breath is always heavy and the waves are wide. By Kriya Yoga technique, breath can be suspended. Before entering into the system, breath is of non-atomic nature. On entering in the system, it splits in to five elements.

******

Cosmos contains more of the sky element. Breath of cosmos emerging out of the self churning of the nameless void is called life force. In Sri vidya, it is called "Viswakundilini". It is breath of all. Cosmic life force is the breath of universe. During interaction of individual breath and cosmic breath, life force flows through Sushumna. Breath is both centre and circumference. The expansion of the centre into a circle of the breath is universe.

******

When vacuumed is created in the system i.e. when there is no breath; it is the state of vacation of breath. Then only the spirit charges the void in the system and divine energy appears. Turiya is vacuumed state i.e. void stateless state during meditation. In this vacuumed state, Udana Prana is generated and corrects the system and makes it healthy. Udana Prana is life force. This creates peace, bliss and joy in the system. Breath can be one's own Guru and gives proper direction, when needed.

******

Mind is conquered by life force energy. It is produced by breath; it is the secret of breath. Life force is also Annarasa. One can live on life force without taking solid food. Generally for a common man only one half of breath goes to Annahata and remaining half is returned without any function.

******

From void i.e. elemental sky cosmic life force is born. It gives birth to atom to mahat to wind to fire to water to earth to vegetable kingdom and then to unicellular organism.

******

Basically void becomes five elements by throbbing and then transforms to Mahabhutas, which descend to every atom of the body; at heart it is air; at manipura it is fire; at swadhistanam it is water; and at mooladhara it is earth. In void they all are woven as Jadha/stable before any transformation. The deep secret of breath is from void to void.

******

It is wonderful to know and practice to take breath from mouth; to store it in naval centre; and then empty it and create total vacuumed. This process of breathing reduces the body heat and makes it cool. If there is pain in the hands, breath must be stored in Vishudhi chakra for some time. In general stored breath is to be moved to location where ever there is pain. In case of bulging out of stomach, sunnayaka/vacuumed of breath through Manipura is to be maintained; for problem in any part of the body, life force to be created in the body, and then after bringing this life force on the tip of fingers, it should be sent to the effected part, where cure is needed. Breath stored in Muladhara, tackles the problem of kidney and lower organs; at swadhistanam stored breath tackles the digestion problems; at manipura stored breath cures stomach pain issues.

******

If right nostril is blocked then problems of right side of the body are piled up, and if left nostril is jammed/blocked then problems of organs located at left side occur. In general exit of the breath shall be elongated to cure the body from various diseases. Tranquil breath removes miseries of life. Basically one must observe rhythm, elongate breath with equal-distribution of storing and vacating of breath for good health.

******

Listening of reverberations of own breath coupled with divine melody is Inner Nada. It is called Antarnadanu -sandhana. In AUM, A stands for earthiness, U stands for Watery and M for Light. Crescent on Aum is Prana and dot (.) is for Akasa. The sequence for descending order is from infinite to void to sky to Prana to Light to Water to Earth.

******

When breath flows from right nostril, it is termed as vertical breath i.e. from Brahm Nadi. When it flows from left nostril, it is termed as horizontal breath i.e. from Indira Nadi. Breath flowing from both nostrils equally (in and out) is called tranquil breath. It is Ekatara breath that creates vacuumed or void in the system and strengthens it. Taking breath from both the nostrils simultaneously indicates the breakage of triangle of the Karmas. This situation/aspect is like Bindu of Sri chakra where both Shiva and Shakti exist together.

******

Sandhya when it is manifested, it is Maya/illusion, and when it is un-manifested, it is Lolita. Breath is Maya. Cessation of breath indicates the presence of God. Mind cannot be at one place even in presence of one breath. Creating Vacuumed by taking away the breath renders mind concentration. Even this cannot be adequately achieved by suspension of breath. Silence of mind cannot be achieved in presence of even the mildest breath. Prana and life force must exit from Sahasrara for perfect silence and mind control. Also, breath/Prana must pass through Sushumna Nadi and must merge with light for absolute silence.

******

If the breath is kept or it rests beyond Dahara Chakra, at Ajana or near to the soul, the decay of the body is very slow. If breath is below Dahara Chakra, decay of body is very fast.

******

The movement of breath as Prana to Apana is horizontal breath and vertical movement of Prana and Apana through Sushumana up to Ajna is vertical divine breath. At Ajna it is called Pratyagatma but at Sahasrara it is termed as Sada Siva. At Unmani Chakra when Pratyagatma loses its cognizance of identity with Supernal than breath has no role to play as light; or as wind; or as other element; like water or earth etc. On its vertical journey, breath must merge at every Chakra; so that at Sahasrara it remains as pure light only; and get easily merge with Supernal.

******

33

Some Deep Mystic Thoughts

Shiva joins Shakti or Shakti joins Shiva, no body knows. But, if one can catch hold of Shakti, he has Shiva also.

******

The sun is called the destroyer of darkness, but how and when did sun perceive any darkness? Day and night are the same for the sun; for the sun there is no night; for pure water, there is no salt; one, who is awake, there is no sleep; in presence of fire, Camphor cannot remain. Finally, when He is seen, both worshipper and object of worship vanish.

******

Self is absolute silence. The attempt to describe the self is like trying to express silence with a Brass-Band.

******

Any type of knowledge is bondage for the self-realization. Intellectual knowledge is a relative knowledge. It is just the basic preparation for self-realization. For absolute knowledge, the aid of some other kind of knowledge is needed i.e. the knowledge to know it self. All other will be nothing but just ignorance.

******

It is mystic to know that if the extinguisher of a light is extinguished along with light, then who knows that there was no light; if a person ceased to be during the period of sleep, then who would know that he was in sound sleep; in life to know nothing, one has to become nothing; if dark person stands in darkness, no body can perceive; still he certainly exists and is aware of his existence.

******

If one can see his face without mirror, it means he understands the reality.

******

When even experience dissolves then what is the use of words; in the mirror of words, what is invisible, may be seen; words can liberate self but cannot live with the self; a shadow does not exist where it does not fall, but it also does not exist where it falls; ignorance is, by its very nature is non-existent, then whom should the words destroy; self is the pure knowledge then how the mundane knowledge can know it; the effect of ignorance is ignorance itself; knowledge and ignorance move together; knowledge and ignorance both depend on the word; and when word disappear then nothing remains; every thing is delusion.

******

Self plays happily with himself; the might can imagine every thing except the self; self is self illuminating; there is no other cause for His seeing Himself than Himself; when seer and seen unit then both vanish; whole universe is the luminosity of the self; it is the vibration of the self.

******

Repetition of His divine name with consciousness getting merge in it, is itself a meditation; truly He Himself is every thing; he is the cause of every thing; His name is saver in miseries; no yoga needed if one is merged in His name; when perceiver and perceived are one or become one then mind is redundant/not required.

******

Books Published by Author

Technical Books by Author